Beth Hoffman

RADICAL RELATIONSHIPS

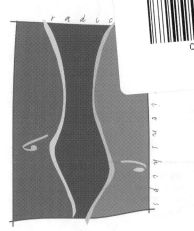

C000145936

THE UNIQUENESS OF
Jesus

Meri MacLeod, Ed.D., Series Editor
Foreword by Walter L. Liefeld, Ph.D.

NAVPRESS
BRINGING TRUTH TO LIFE
NavPress Publishing Group
P.O. Box 35001, Colorado Springs, Colorado 80935

The RADICAL RELATIONSHIPS series is a joint effort of two Navigator ministries—NavPress and Women of Influence (WIN). WIN is a resource ministry encouraging women to make a difference for Christ in the marketplace. More information appears on page 89.

The Navigators is an international Christian organization. Our mission is to reach, disciple, and equip people to know Christ and to make him known through successive generations. We envision multitudes of diverse people in the United States and every other nation who have a passionate love for Christ, live a lifestyle of sharing Christ's love, and multiply spiritual laborers among those without Christ.

NavPress is the publishing ministry of The Navigators. NavPress publications help believers learn biblical truth and apply what they learn to their lives and ministries. Our mission is to stimulate spiritual formation among our readers.

Printed in the United States of America

1 2 3 4 5 6 7 8 9 10 11 12 13 14 15 / 00 99 98 97 96

FOR A FREE CATALOG OF
NAVPRESS BOOKS & BIBLE STUDIES,
CALL 1-800-366-7788 (USA)
or 1-416-499-4615 (CANADA)

FOR INFORMATION ABOUT WIN OR
HELP USING THE RADICAL RELATIONSHIPS SERIES,
CALL 1-719-548-7450

CONTENTS

"RADICAL RELATIONSHIPS studies provide a non-threatening way for men and women of all backgrounds to experience a stimulating discussion of God's Word and to wrestle with the meaning of God's truth for their daily lives."
—Soozi Bolte, broadcast producer, Focus on the Family
(formerly director of women's ministries)

"Our home group has enjoyed the stimulating discussions we have with RADICAL RELATIONSHIPS Bible studies. The design makes it easy for anyone in our couples group to lead a study ."
—Jon and Beth Werner, small-group leaders

"RADICAL RELATIONSHIPS has worked great with the busy schedules of our small-group leaders. These studies take so little preparation and are so easy to use, anyone can be confident in leading a Bible study group."
—Frank Kennedy, small-group coordinator

"These studies have been an exciting discovery for our adult Sunday school. Men and women of all ages experience stimulating discussions around their study of the Bible."
—Margy Price, Christian education director

"RADICAL RELATIONSHIPS was perfect for a Bible study in the hospital with nurses from a wide variety of religious backgrounds."
—Karen Nichols, M.D., physician

Books in the RADICAL RELATIONSHIPS series:

FOREWORD

Whenever I enter a Christian bookstore, I am always impressed with the variety of Bible study guides lining the shelves. We are immensely fortunate to have not only the Bible itself accessible in various translations, but also a variety of reference helps for people of all ages and circumstances. The RADICAL RELATIONSHIPS series, I believe, deserves a prominent place among these publications.

Perhaps the outstanding characteristic of these studies is that they assume both the God-given intelligence of the reader in *understanding* the text and the illumination of the Holy Spirit in *applying* the text. Series editor Meri MacLeod, with whom I have had the pleasure of collaborating in some small way during the development of these books, has drawn upon sound Bible study methods using the tools she gained in earning a doctorate in Christian education at Trinity Evangelical Divinity School. Instead of focusing on one single mode, she has skillfully created an eclectic yet simple approach to allow users to adapt the guide to their particular backgrounds and interests. After many years of experience in small-group Bible studies, I appreciate finding in this series some of the finest elements used in effective methods.

Because the RADICAL RELATIONSHIPS series takes full cognizance of the Bible as literature, it leads us to look at the text in its *context*—literary, historical, and cultural. It starts us with observing the facts, to guard against finding in the text only what we already cherish.

Simply clarifying the "who, what, where, and when" of a passage, however, is not enough. We must move beyond simply observing the text to identifying its inner connections—cause-and-effect, contrast, climax, and so on. This step enables us to think along with the biblical writers in the development of the truth being taught, in the unfolding of the story line, or in whatever other progression (such as poetry) there may be. Here the study design will help us to grasp the intentions of the Holy Spirit in couching these facts in a specific style of literature and with particular purposes paragraph by paragraph.

After understanding the facts and their interconnections, we need to apply the Scripture to our own circumstances. The natural tendency of an earnest seeker is to jump to application before understanding the data and their interconnections. The RADICAL RELATIONSHIPS guides carefully lead us in discerning how to respond to what we have seen and heard while observing and reflecting upon the text.

Although this approach is excellent for personal study, it is particularly fruitful for one-on-one or small-group use. Because the study design is intended to engender *conversation* about the Scriptures rather than simply factual observation, it provides a vehicle for the nurture of "radical relationships" among group participants. These guides were initially developed to provide a tool for women in the marketplace, but I have watched men who were previously hesitant to participate coming alive through the use of these studies. I am impressed with the vigorous discussion they stimulate across lines of gender, age, and personal background—in part because the role of facilitator, or leader, is open to anyone in the group, not just those with the greatest biblical background. The sessions are designed to encourage an open-ended learning experience in a variety of settings, whether a half-hour in a restaurant an hour's discussion during an evening home group. Moreover, since no advance preparation is needed, no one in the group is excluded from discussion — a benefit highly valued by those in the RADICAL RELATIONSHIPS studies I have personally led. In my perception, this feature enhances the study experience because learning takes place in the context of interaction.

As a pastor, I welcome the influence of this series in stimulating dialogue about the Bible and its claims upon our lives. Whether we are babes in the word or long-time readers of it, we are always in need of hearing the Scriptures speak to us afresh — through another's perspective as well as our own. It is my hope that these studies will lead us into deepening relationships as together we seek to know the Lord who so graciously reveals himself in his word.

Walter L. Liefeld, Ph.D.
Professor Emeritus of New Testament, Trinity Evangelical Divinity School
Senior Pastor, Christ Church Lake Forest, Lake Forest, Illinois

ACKNOWLEDGMENTS

The RADICAL RELATIONSHIPS series began as a dream of Bible studies that would fit the demanding lifestyle of men and women today. Through many years in ministry it became clear to me that men and women deeply desire to spend time in Scripture, but they struggle to find Bible studies with the right combination of flexible structure and stimulating experience in God's Word.

During 1990 and 1991, I began noticing the numerous calls we were receiving in our office asking for Bible studies that would work for the unique needs of the marketplace. It became increasingly evident that there was a hunger for a Bible study that men and women could comfortably use with their colleagues in their places of work.

With the help of a team from across the country, I began the initial design of RADICAL RELATIONSHIPS. In 1992 the field test edition was printed, and copies found their way across the U.S. and several places overseas. Hundreds of men and women used those field test studies in small and large companies, hospitals, neighborhood groups, government offices, university campuses, church Bible classes, small groups in homes, and in church planting. These experiences provided me with regular and insightful feedback, and an enthusiastic cry for more RADICAL RELATIONSHIPS studies!

Bringing my vision to a larger audience could not have happened without the enthusiastic support of John Eames, publisher of NavPress. I am deeply grateful for his vision and eagerness to publish a new design in Bible studies. Various members of the Women of Influence ministry, especially the national director, Mim Pain, have made an invaluable contribution as they critiqued the many rough drafts. Patiently guiding us through the production process have been Kathy Yanni and Karen Lee-Thorp. I am very thankful for their listening ear and creative editoral work on our behalf.

The design of these studies has truly been developed within the context of a community of believers. My continuing prayer is that RADICAL RELATIONSHIPS studies will stimulate small groups of men and women, young and old, who will come to know each other more fully as together they come to know the Lord Jesus Christ more deeply.

Meri MacLeod, Ed.D, Series Editor

P.S. I continue to welcome your feedback and ideas for future RADICAL RELATIONSHIPS studies. Tell me how you're using these studies. You may phone me at (719)548-7450, or fax to (719)548-7453.

INTRODUCTION

Conversations about spirituality are common today. Questions like, "What do you think about angels?" or "How was your meditation class last night?" can be heard as people begin to share their growing hunger for a spiritual experience. At one time, religion and spirituality were assumed to be unnecessary and irrelevant, but today more and more people are pursuing some kind of spiritual experience.

In this context of spiritual hunger, people are more willing to investigate first hand who Jesus Christ is. Many carry distorted pictures of Jesus and have rarely looked at eyewitness accounts of what Jesus really did and said. These studies offer an opportunity to invite your friends, who may know little about Jesus, to discover some of the things that make him unique from all other religious leaders. Explore his remarkable compassion for an unknown widow or his power to heal a child. Ponder his supernatural power to forgive sin and to raise the dead. Reflect on the confession of worship blurted by a follower who sees Jesus in person after his resurrection.

The eight studies in this book are taken from the four eyewitness accounts, the Gospels, which have been carefully preserved since their writing. These studies will help those who are new followers of Jesus or for those who are seeking to discover Jesus for the first time. And these studies can also encourage those who have been Christians for many years to rediscover the remarkable things that Jesus did and to reflect on their own faith in him.

As your friends grow hungry to know more about Jesus, another book in this series, *Jesus on Relationships*, will be a great way to continue their investigation into the person of Jesus Christ.

RADICAL RELATIONSHIPS studies offer an added richness as you experience these studies with a variety of people—teenagers and adults, men and women—for each person brings insight from the Holy Spirit to expand our individual understanding of the person of Jesus. For each of us, our understanding of God is limited. But we can come together around Scripture and discover as the Holy Spirit speaks through each one, a more complete understanding of who God really is. RADICAL RELATIONSHIPS studies help create a learning community around God's Word. You can rely on the work of the Holy Spirit in each believer to reveal God's truth, to teach and to convict.

Chapter One
CONVERSATIONAL BIBLE STUDY: A NEW APPROACH

What makes RADICAL RELATIONSHIPS studies different?

- People **talk together** about Bible discoveries, rather than hunting for fill-in-the-blank answers.

- **No preparation** is needed by people participating in these studies.

- Each study is **self-contained**, so people who miss a week can continue to participate fully.

- **Anyone** can take a turn at leading the study/discussion with the user-friendly discussion guides.

- **Seekers have the freedom** to encounter Jesus' words and actions through a lively discussion of insights and discoveries.

- **Sixteen complete** discussion guides: eight 30-minutes studies and eight 60-minute studies.

- Study method is so **transferable** people can do the same study with friends after experiencing it in a RADICAL RELATIONSHIPS group.

- People learn good **Bible study habits** by experiencing them in each study.

- People make profound biblical discoveries through **personal digging** into the Scriptures and **open discussion** in community with others.

- The **flexible** format and style work for busy people and in **any setting**: home, office, Sunday school class, one-to-one discipleship, adults, collegians, teens, etc.

STUDIES THAT DEEPEN RELATIONSHIPS

Relationships seem to be on everyone's mind. People want to talk with others about meaningful things and with deep-felt emotion. They long to deepen their relationship with God, or at least with the spiritual side of themselves if they don't believe in God. The Bible is full of stories and teachings about relationships—people relating to people and God relating to people.

The RADICAL RELATIONSHIPS series is designed to encourage people to talk together about what they discover in the Bible concerning relationships with God and with people. *The Uniqueness of Jesus* explores biblical stories from the four Gospels which illustrate why Jesus Christ is different from other religious leaders. Passages explored will unfold profound insights for committed believers and seekers alike. Conversational Bible studies will expand relationships and reveal new truths.

CONVERSATIONAL BIBLE STUDY STYLE

The format and style of these studies may be very different from your previous experiences. There is no one "teacher" who expounds correct information, no fill-in-the-blank questions to answer, and nothing people must prepare in order to participate. People can dig into the Bible for themselves and share their personal insights in a lively conversational discussion. Everyone is a learner-teacher.

Two discussion formats are provided. One is a 30-minute discussion guide that works well for people with limited schedules, such as for breakfast or lunch meetings. The other is a discussion guide for 60 minutes or more, usable in more flexible settings. Both formats take you through the same three steps of the conversational Bible study process:

Step 1 — Research for Facts

Step 2 — Review for Meaning

Step 3 — Respond for Life

The format and discussion can be easily tailored to a few friends or any size group. How? Consider how Jan, Bryan, and Patricia used *The Uniqueness of Jesus*. . . .

JAN AND BRYAN'S HOME GROUP OF NEW AND COMMITTED BELIEVERS

Jan, a realtor, spent her lunchtime Monday browsing Christian bookstores for Bible study materials. She and Bryan, a research chemist, had been leading a group from their community church in their home for nearly a year, and they were about due for something new to study. Jan had been in a lot of Bible studies over the years, and she was secretly tired of the fill-in-the-blank studies she had been using. She longed for a study where people could wrestle with real-life issues and explore how Scripture related to everyday life. It would be great if the people would think and talk more, too, not just lean on Bryan's talent for teaching. When Jan happened upon the RADICAL RELATIONSHIPS series, she had a sense it was just what she and the people in her group needed.

"Look!" she showed Bryan excitedly that evening, while the dinner dishes waited in the sink. "These conversational Bible studies are so turn-key, we could even share the leadership with Dale and Linda, or even Greg could repeat the same study with his group of guys who meet for breakfast."

"Do you think so?" Bryan was hopeful. Pastor Steve had been nudging them to look for ways to encourage leadership in others so their home group would reach out in a wider influence. "You know what else I like about this," he said as he thumbed through the guide. "When you study this way, you'll actually be learning great Bible study methods without realizing it. Pastor Steve will love this — a Bible discussion guide that makes it easy for anyone in our home group to lead and encourages good study habits, too. And we'll actually be talking together about the meaning of Scripture."

Bryan was right about Pastor Steve. He and Jan ran RADICAL RELATIONSHIPS by the pastor for his opinion, and as expected, Pastor Steve lit up. "Let me know how the first study goes," he said. "I think some of the other home groups might want to know about this."

Jan and Bryan knew the people very well who were in their home group. Many had shared a desire to do Bible studies at work or with friends but felt inadequate or afraid they didn't know enough. After studying the book they decided to get a copy of *The Uniqueness of Jesus* for each person. Once people see the simple one-page step-by-step discussion guides, the great discussion questions provided, and the system of putting questions on a "Future Study List" (page 20), they know everyone would feel capable of facilitating these conversational Bible studies.

In planning for the first study, Jan and Bryan needed only to think through:

➤ Who will be coming to the study?

➤ Where and when will we meet?

➤ How long will the discussion be?

"'Where and when'—that's easy," said Jan. "It's at our house, every second and fourth Tuesday night."

"'Who' is pretty simple, too," said Bryan. "Our group has both new and committed believers, we know each other pretty well, and there are usually ten or twelve of us on any given night."

"For 'How long' we can choose thirty minutes or sixty minutes—sixty is about right for us, since we usually enjoy a good discussion."

Bryan and Jan had a comfortable setting for a conversational Bible study: a regular group of familiar faces, all believers, in a quiet place with no distractions, with plenty of time to talk. Leading a *Uniqueness of Jesus* discussion would be easy for them. But *The Uniqueness of Jesus* would be just as effective in Patricia's quite different situation.

PATRICIA'S STUDY FOR SEEKERS AT WORK

Patricia worked in human resources for a medium-size corporation. She had facilitated business meetings before, yet had never led a Bible study. But at a seminar, a friend in her human resource network mentioned she had been leading discussions from *The Uniqueness of Jesus* at her office.

"How do you get away with it?" was Patricia's first question. Teaching religion at the office was strictly prohibited.

"But I'm not teaching anything," explained Barbara. "People just read the Bible passage photocopied on a study sheet and talk about what they observe. When I throw in my two cents, it's just as one of the group. If they want to know more about what I believe about God, we talk about it privately, off-site, at lunch or something."

"And people actually come, week after week?"

"Well, we do it only once a month. And people come and go. People are busy—travel, meetings, stuff like that. But you know, lots of people are interested in discussing spirituality these days, if you don't push your own views down their throats. It's more like a conversation."

Patricia had actually talked about spirituality with a couple of women at her company, and she wondered if they might be interested in discussing something from the Bible if things were low-key and there were no strings attached. So she bought a copy of *The Uniqueness of Jesus* and began planning how a group might work. She asked herself the same three questions Jan and Bryan had asked themselves.

Barbara's group met in a conference room at her office, but where Patricia worked, the conference rooms were always booked, and she really wanted to keep a low profile. So Patricia decided to invite her colleagues Evangelina and Glenna to discuss a RADICAL RELATIONSHIPS conversational study during lunch at Clyde's, where they could get a booth and be in and out in one hour. She was nervous about how to best invite her friends, but Evangelina and Glenna were intrigued (neither had ever even opened a Bible in their lives), and Glenna even said Maureen, the manager of Customer Service, would be interested in something like that. Patricia enthusiastically said, "Bring her along."

So, while Jan and Bryan's group had studied the Bible together often, Patricia had three women whose spiritual beliefs were unknown, who probably knew little or nothing about the Bible, and who didn't know each other well, if at all. She had no more than 30 minutes for the Bible discussion itself and all the distractions of a restaurant to contend with. Patricia was no Bible expert, but she had an ally: the Holy Spirit.

The RADICAL RELATIONSHIPS series is founded upon the belief that when receptive people honestly explore the Scripture, the Holy Spirit will take responsibility to be their teacher. God's Word is alive, and the Spirit is alive, so whenever people come together around the Bible, God will be active. So Patricia could lead the discussion as a learner among learners and a partner with God, expecting the Holy Spirit to prompt insights and discoveries for herself and her friends.

BRYAN AND JAN PREPARE FOR THEIR STUDY

Bryan and Jan read through "Leading a Study Step by Step" (pages 21-26) and then reviewed the 60-minute discussion guide for Luke 1:26-38 (pages 28-29). The guide gave them several options such as whether to open in prayer, a variety of discussion questions and several options for concluding the session. They decided to open and close with prayer, and highlighted the questions in Step Two and the conclusion option in Step Three that seemed to best suit their group. Bryan also liked the "Troubleshooter's Guide to Effective Discussions" (pages 79-83), which gave excellent guidance for difficulties their home group had already encountered.

PATRICIA PREPARES FOR HER STUDY

Patricia carefully studied "Leading a Study Step by Step" but spent more time in chapter 7, "Using Radical Relationships Studies in Special Settings" (pages 83-87).This chapter gave her tips for using these studies in multicultural settings (Evangelina was from a prominent Latino family), with people in the marketplace, and with seekers. Having a discussion guide designed just for a 30-minute study was extremely helpful. She highlighted the questions she felt would best help the group unfold meaning from the passage and chose a Respond for Life option which seemed best for her friends and the restaurant setting. She decided to neither open nor close in prayer since for her seeker friends this was primarily a discussion time similar to other lunchtime discussion meetings. Patricia was confident the Holy Spirit had heard her prayers before leaving her office. She knew he would keep important discoveries made during the discussion in the hearts of her colleagues even if they couldn't close in prayer.

PATRICIA'S LUNCH MEETING

At 11:45 a.m. on the appointed day, Patricia met Evangelina, Glenna, and Maureen at Clyde's. Having beaten the lunch rush, the four women selected the most spacious booth. They chatted about work and Evangelina's kids until after they ordered, then Patricia gently gave focus to the discussion.

Because the four were just getting acquainted with each other, Patricia thought an ice-breaker would help them feel comfortable sharing more freely once they got around to the Bible study. She had come with an activity she had experienced at a recent seminar. On the table she laid out four strips each of four colors of paper. The colored strips represented four different facets of personality. The red strips represented "risk-taker," green was for "thinker," gold for "reader," and blue for "fun-loving." Patricia asked each woman to select one or two of the four colors that she felt reflected her personality. After everyone had selected one or two strips, Patricia asked each woman to tell why she had chosen *one* of the colors for herself. She went first, explaining that she had chosen gold for "reader" because she loved to read, whether it was a new mystery, the newspaper, or a biography. Following her lead, the other three women shared something about themselves as prompted by the colored strips.

This kind of an ice-breaker helped the women talk about themselves on a neutral, up-beat, low-threat subject. She didn't want them focusing on their jobs because job categories tend to rank people. Evangelina might feel intimidated to be in a group with Maureen the personnel manager. But on the subject of personality, everyone could relate and had something to say.

The ice-breaker took about five minutes, and then Patricia pulled out five sheets from her portfolio. One was a photocopy of her 30-minute discussion guide for Luke 1:26-38 (pages 30-31); the other four were copies of the Bible Study and Background Information sheet for each woman. (See pages 11 and 62-63.) There was no need to risk embarrassment by bringing Bibles to a restaurant because the Bible passage was printed right on the study sheets. Patricia had also brought colored pens for everyone.

The food arrived quickly, so everyone took a few minutes to eat before Patricia began the discussion. Last night, she had highlighted parts of the To Begin section on her discussion guide.

First, Patricia said, "We're going to be investigating a passage from the Bible using a conversational discussion format. This is an investigative approach which can be used to analyze any written material. A passage from the Bible is printed on our sheets. It will help if we understand something about the context from which the passage was taken, and a little about the culture of Jesus' day. Take a look at the Background Information on Luke 1:26-38. I'll read it aloud."

Next, she read through the Discussion Guidelines on the bottom of the sheet. The guidelines set the groundrules, such as "Each person respects the value of others' insights." A couple of the women nodded—the guidelines reassured them that they were not in for an indoctrination session. One woman said, "Good, now I know what's expected of me."

Patricia went on: "Now take three or four minutes on your own to read the Bible passage. As you read, think about these two questions in the left margin: '*Who* is involved in the story?' and '*What* is going on?' You can jot notes if you want, or circle words, or underline—whatever works for you. You can see there's room in the margin on the left for notes. Using different color pens helps some people."

A few minutes passed while the women ate and read. Maureen and Glenna wrote and circled; Evangelina didn't. After three or four minutes, Patricia said, "Let me interrupt. To lay a foundation for our discussion, let's restate the facts by describing who is involved and what is happening." There was silence for a moment. Patricia just waited for them to collect their thoughts.

Soon Evangelina responded: "This is really different. An angel talking to a woman? I don't know what to think. What does this really mean?"

Patricia flinched inwardly, but Barbara had prepared her to expect anything. She was glad Evangelina felt free to be honest, and she knew questions like these open people up to grapple with the Bible, get involved, look closely at the passage, and listen to each other. She was committed to let the Holy Spirit be at work, so she turned the questions back to the group: "Thanks, Evangelina. Those are important questions. What do the rest of you think? Can we find helpful facts or answers from this passage?"

Glenna began to note all the different people who were mentioned in the passage, and Maureen chimed in with how unusual their interaction was. A lively discussion followed, and Patricia actually had to interrupt when their time was up. She didn't want anyone to avoid coming next time because the meeting made them late. So she broke in, "We need to wrap this up and get back to work, but it sure was fun hearing everyone's perspective. Is anyone interested in doing this again?" As they left the restaurant, all three, including Maureen, said they wanted to tackle another Bible discussion next week, same time, same place.

Jan and Bryan's Evening

Things went just as well at Jan and Bryan's house. Some people raised eyebrows when Bryan introduced the new study by saying the group was going to do the hard work instead of him this week. But their enthusiasm rose when they got into the study and found the "work" both enjoyable and profound. Who, What, and How turned out to be the most significant Research questions; the group didn't bother discussing the others. The discussion questions under Review provoked a lively interchange after several unique observations on contrasts. Bryan hardly had to say anything, and instead of answering questions as he usually did, he wrote down some that went on the "Future Study List." But for the most part, the group was able to answer its own questions because everyone kept digging in the passage for new discoveries. And people were actually eager to Respond—there was quite a bit of scribbling during the period of reflection. Over coffee afterward, one man confided to Jan the ultimate compliment: "I've heard a lot of sermons on this passage, but tonight's discussion gave me some challenges and insights I've never seen before!"

Chapter Two
KEYS TO SUCCESS

RADICAL RELATIONSHIPS conversational Bible study is designed to stimulate personal discovery from a Bible passage and interactive discussion that wrestles with the meanings of Scripture for today. Your role as discussion leader, to encourage the exchange of ideas and observations, is a central element of these unique studies.

FIVE KEYS TO SUCCESS
After two years of field-testing with a wide variety of people, five keys to effective RADICAL RELATIONSHIPS studies have clearly emerged.

1. Don't skip lightly over gathering the facts in Step One. Valid observations and authentic meanings discussed in Step Two depend on a good understanding of the facts from Step One. Most people find it more enjoyable to skip right to explaining what they think the passage means. But the interpretations of a passage can become unreliable when sufficient time is not given to gleaning the basic facts. Since every word of Scripture is significant, time sharing the discoveries of key facts is essential for a rich study. People feel more comfortable sharing the basic facts of a passage when you explain that the goal of Step One is to find answers to the fact-finding questions and lay a foundation for the Bible study. This leads to a good discussion in Step Two, the discovery of meanings from the passage.

2. Create an atmosphere of trust, respect, and acceptance. It is important to build trust among people so that everyone becomes comfortable sharing their thoughts and discoveries from the passage, even if those discoveries may seem insignificant or different. As the discussion leader, your facial expressions and tone of voice need to convey respect and acceptance for each observation expressed, even when it seems unusual or irrelevant to you. For example, one affirming way of responding is to warmly say, "That's an interesting observation. Explain how you saw that in this passage?" For additional responses to unusual comments without closing down the discussion, turn to page 79.

Trust is also a matter of knowing one another, especially on an introductory level. If you are using these studies with people who do not know each other, consider using a simple get-acquainted exercise, such as the one used by Patricia on page 16. Once people have shared familiar things about themselves, they are more ready to share their ideas or observations from the Bible passage.

3. Keep your preparation simple. Your role is to facilitate the exchange of ideas, not to expound as an expert. Your preparation should *not* include in-depth study of the Bible passage. Over-preparation can make you too eager to share your knowledge and stifle other people's open sharing. You will be seen as the "prepared expert" rather than the discussion facilitator. Less knowledgeable people will not want to risk sharing for fear they will be "wrong." Remember, you can count on the Holy Spirit to reveal insights and important teachings.

Therefore, simply read over the passage on the study sheet for familiarity. Then on your discussion guide, highlight which discussion questions you want to use from point four in Step Two and which option you want to use in Step Three. Chapter 3 will lead you through this brief preparation.

4. Reviewing the Discussion Guidelines helps everyone know what's expected of them.
For the first few studies, or whenever anyone new comes to a study, review the Discussion Guidelines on the Bible Study and Background Information sheet. It helps to ask, "Are you comfortable with these?" If people have never done Bible study in a group, they will be grateful to know the groundrules.

DISCUSSION GUIDELINES
Discussions go better when each person:

1. Respects the value of everyone's observations or insights

2. Allows everyone opportunity to speak, if they so choose

3. Focuses the discussion on the passage being studied

4. Shares freely, but refrains from correcting or giving advice

5. Keeps all personal sharing confidential

6. Puts unanswered questions on the "Future Study List"

5. Using a "Future Study List" means everyone shares a learner/teacher role in the study.
RADICAL RELATIONSHIPS studies are designed to encourage everyone to learn from one another, sharing the role of teacher. As people study the passage privately they share the teacher role by talking about their individual observations or insights. The RADICAL RELATIONSHIPS method encourages each person to dig for themselves and think in new ways about the Bible passage. As a result, questions may be raised which do not seem to be answered in the passage. As the facilitator, first encourage everyone to look for answers in the passage; do not answer the question as the "expert." If no answer is found, tell the people you will place the question on the "Future Study List" and continue your discussion. Space is provided at the bottom of each Discussion Guide for questions that will need to be studied further. At the conclusion of that study, ask for a volunteer to research the questions on the list, or agree together to save all the questions on the list until the end of the series. Refer volunteers to Bible dictionaries, commentaries, handbooks, or encyclopedias found in most church libraries. The volunteer can bring the book to the study and read selections from it.

Chapter Three
LEADING A STUDY
STEP BY STEP

For each of the eight studies in this book there is a Bible Study and Background Information sheet (see chapter 5) plus the 30- or 60-minute Discussion Guides (chapter 4) for the person leading the study.

The Discussion Guides are designed to help you lead a discussion with just a few minutes of preparation. Each Discussion Guide includes: (1) step-by-step instructions for guiding people through the three steps of the conversational Bible study process, (2) additional discussion questions, and (3) suggestions for beginning and ending your study. There are separate Discussion Guides for 60-minute and 30-minute formats. These guides enable anyone, especially those who do not consider themselves to be Bible teachers, to effectively lead a RADICAL RELATIONSHIPS conversational study.

The following pages take you through a typical RADICAL RELATIONSHIPS study from start to finish.

PREPARING TO LEAD THE STUDY

Only the discussion leader needs to prepare for a RADICAL RELATIONSHIPS study. And your preparation is very brief! Here are the five simple steps of preparation:

1. Pray for your time together. Ask the Lord to prepare the hearts of all who will come and to use his Spirit to bring his Word alive. Pray also for yourself that you will be relaxed and eager to learn from each person who will participate in the study.

2. Determine which time frame you will use, 60-minute or 30-minute, and select the appropriate Discussion Guide. Read through the Discussion Guide for an overview of how the study is designed.

3. Become familiar with the Research for Facts questions of Step One and the Review for Meaning questions of Step Two. See pages 22-24 in this chapter.

4. Read briefly the Bible passage printed on the sheet.

5. Choose the discussion questions in Step Two and the option for Step Three that best suits the people who will participate in the study.

USING THE DISCUSSION GUIDE

TO BEGIN

At the top of each Discussion Guide are the first four things to do as you begin a study:

1. Look at the Bible Study and Background Information sheet.

2. Read the Background Information then review the Discussion Guidelines with everyone.

3. Explain that the study involves a three-step process: Research for Facts, Review for Meaning and Respond for Life.

4. Pray, if appropriate for your setting and the people involved.

As the group becomes more familiar with the style of these conversational studies, you will need to spend less time explaining the three steps of the RADICAL RELATIONSHIPS method or reviewing the Discussion Guidelines. *But in the beginning all four steps will be very important.* Always review the three-step process and Discussion Guidelines when new people come to the study.

When leading a study with new people for the first time, you may find the following sample introduction useful: "On the study sheet you have just received, you'll notice some background information for the passage we will be studying. I'll read this aloud for us. As you follow along, feel free to mark any part that seems especially interesting to you." After reading the background information, introduce the Discussion Guidelines: "On the bottom of this page you'll notice discussion guidelines for our study. These are designed to help our discussion go smoothly, so I'll read them for us as you follow along." Understanding these guidelines helps each person know the groundrules and feel comfortable with what's expected of them during the study. After reading them you can ask, "Is everyone comfortable with these?"

Next, tell the people the three steps of the RADICAL RELATIONSHIPS conversational study process. You may decide it is best not to pray because of your public office or restaurant setting.

STEP ONE: RESEARCH FOR FACTS

The goal in Step One is for you and each person in the study to read the Scripture passage individually and discover answers to the questions listed in the left margin of the Bible Study and Background Information sheet. If you are using the 30-minute format, you may find it speeds things up to read the passage aloud before doing the individual study. Discoveries may be written in the left margin, underlined, circled, or marked with different color pens, but you may not find answers to all six questions. *Step One is crucial to the process of studying Scripture inductively and to finding meanings in Step Two.* Thoroughness in Step One helps avoid the trap of drawing conclusions based on what you have heard about a passage, or on what you think a passage says. You will be surprised at the insights gained when you begin with careful discovery of the facts, especially those facts easily overlooked. The author of each passage of Scripture has carefully selected specific facts to communicate the message. The challenge in Bible study is to discover the facts and ponder why just those particular facts were included.

1. Explain Step One by pointing out the Research for Facts questions in the left margin of the Bible passage, and tell people the goal listed in Step One. Become familiar with the expanded descriptions of the Research for Facts questions listed below so you can supplement the briefer definitions provided on the study sheet under Step One.

RESEARCH FOR FACTS

◣ **WHO is involved?** Who are the people talking? Who is listening? Who is doing something?

◣ **WHAT is happening?** What is going on between people? What are the big events of the story?

◣ **WHAT is said?** What is Jesus or God saying? What do others say?

◣ **HOW do people relate or respond?** How do people interact, react, talk, listen?

◣ **WHEN?** When does the story take place? Is there a sequence of events or timing?

◣ **WHERE did this happen?** What location is described? Does the action move from place to place?

(*Note:* The 30-minute discussion guide directs you to use only the first three questions because of the limited time.)

2. Read the Bible Passage. Allow several minutes for everyone to read the Bible passage and make observations to the Research for Facts questions. Note the suggested time for this step on the 60-minute and the 30-minute Discussion Guides. Encourage people to mark their sheets in any way that enhances their study. Explain that marking the study sheet can reveal important patterns or emphases. If you are using the 30-minute format, it will save time to read the passage aloud for everyone, then invite people to look back through the passage for significant facts.

3. Discuss your findings. Encourage a spontaneous conversation about facts discovered. It will tend to stifle discussion if you take a rigid approach by going down the list of questions in a strict order. Remember, there may not be answers for all questions. Invite people to share discoveries in any order, what they saw as the significant facts. The Discussion Guide provides the following opening questions to begin the discussion of Step One: "What did you discover about who is involved and what is happening?" or "What did you discover about how people are responding?"

4. Watch your time and move to Step Two even if all facts are not mentioned.

5. Cautions for Step One. Guard against three hinderances to effective discussion and discovery: (1) Someone may immediately share personal applications of the Bible passage while skipping over the facts. You can simply acknowledge the insight and suggest that the discussion focus on the facts of the passage, saving applications for later. (2) A question may be raised for which no one finds an answer in the passage. Affirm the question's importance and record it on the "Future Study List," then return to discussing the facts of the passage. See page 20 in chapter 2. (3) You may be tempted to "fill in" for silence. Be patient with silence when you first ask people to share their discoveries. Some people need time to formulate a response; others wonder if it's safe to speak up. People need time to become comfortable with examining a passage for the facts. Gently reaffirm the importance of Step One, and encourage people with the value of their observations even when they seem so "basic." On occasion, you may begin sharing some facts you observed, *being careful* not to list them all.

Step Two: REVIEW FOR MEANING

Everyone will read the Bible passage individually a second time. The goal now is to discover meaning by using the analysis questions in the Review for Meaning column. As discoveries are made regarding repetition, contrast, comparison, etc., the central meaning of the passage will begin to come to light. As in Step One, encourage people to make notes directly on their sheet by writing in the right margin, circling words, underlining, or marking particular words with colored pens.

1. Explain Step Two. Direct the group's attention to the right margin of the Bible passage where the questions are listed. Become familiar with the following descriptions so you can expand on the briefer definitions in the right margin.

REVIEW FOR MEANING

◢ **What REPETITION?** Identify words or phrases used more than once in the same passage. Repetition is one of the author's ways of emphasizing something. Repetition may include key words.

◢ **What CONTRASTS/OPPOSITES?** Look for the association of opposites. The author wishes to highlight something by showing that it is different from something else. Words which often indicate contrast in a passage are "but," "nevertheless," "although," and "yet." Also notice characters in the story who act in contrasting ways (e.g., disciples versus Jesus).

➤ **What COMPARISON/SIMILARITIES?** Look for people, ideas, or objects which share some likeness with another object, idea, or person., or two things that are similar in some way. For example, "As the Father has loved me, so have I loved you" (John 15:9). Words which can indicate comparison are "as," "just as," "so also," and "likewise."

➤ **What KEY WORDS?** What key words seem important? What central theme do they recall?

➤ **What SIGNIFICANCE or IMPLICATIONS?** What significant meanings do you see in the passage? What are some implications for our lives today?

It is likely that not all five of these questions will be relevant to every passage.

2. Re-read the Bible passage. Allow several minutes for everyone to study the Bible passage again and record observations to the analysis questions. Note the suggested time for this step on the 60-minute and the 30-minute Discussion Guides. Encourage people who wish to make notes directly on their sheet by writing in the right margin, circling words, underlining, or marking particular words with colored pens. This is especially effective for discovering contrast, comparison, or repetition patterns in the passage.

3. Discuss your findings. As in Step One, encourage conversation about what each person has found to be *significant* observations for them. It is not necessary to thoroughly discuss repetition, then contrast, etc. To keep the discussion within suggested time limits, you may need to focus on just a few key insights. Allow for a spontaneous conversation of discoveries rather than a methodical reporting of all repetition found, then all contrast found, and so on. The Discussion Guide provides the following opening questions to begin the sharing of Step Two: "What repetition, contrast, or comparison did you discover? Why are these important to the meaning of the passage for you?"

To enhance your discussion and encourage wrestling with key aspects of each passage, several additional discussion questions have been provided in Step Two. It is likely that there are more questions than you will have time to discuss. Part of your preparation for each study will be to select those discussion questions that you expect to be most helpful.

4. Conclude Step Two. Since Step Three is so important, graciously conclude Step Two with adequate time remaining for people to respond in Step Three.

STEP THREE: RESPOND FOR LIFE

The goal of Step Three is to invite people to reflect on the meaning of the study for their own lives and to ponder possible responses. This step is the culmination of the inductive study process since it involves putting the insights gained from the Bible into personal use for everyday living. It is a response to what the Spirit of God has revealed in the passage or spoken through the sharing of others.

Each Discussion Guide includes several options for Step Three. You can invite people to share their personal responses, or allow time for everyone to reflect on the passage privately by writing their responses in the bottom margin of their sheet. This is a key moment to trust the Holy Spirit to lead you and work in others.

The option you choose in Step Three may be influenced by the people in the study, the setting, or what has been shared. For example, if your study involves primarily believers who know each other well, your response discussion may become quite personal. If you are meeting with professional women or men in an office setting, some of whom do not know each other and perhaps one or two who may not be committed followers of Jesus Christ, then you will want to be low-key and careful about sharing personal responses. The best choice for seekers is often either Option One or simply inviting people to acknowledge a new discovery about Jesus. If your discussion focuses on a theme, questions from Option Two or a response question you create yourself may be most helpful.

To Close

Each Discussion Guide suggests two elements for the close of the study: (1) pray together if appropriate for the setting and people in the study, and (2) agree on the time, place, and discussion leader for the next study.

Future Study List

At the bottom of each Discussion Guide is a space to list any questions that arise in your study that cannot be answered from the passage. You can keep track of these questions by listing them here. (See page 20.)

> *Note:* If you are leading a study with seekers who may not be ready to purchase a book, you have the option of photocopying the Bible Study and Background Information sheets. Limited permission is given on page 11.

Chapter Four

30- AND 60-MINUTE
DISCUSSION GUIDES
FOR LEADERS

A UNIQUE BEGINNING
Luke 1:26-38
⇊

TO BEGIN
(allow 5 minutes)

1. Look at the Bible Study and Background Information sheet for Luke 1:26-38.

2. Read the Background Information, then review the Discussion Guidelines with everyone.

3. Explain that the study/discussion involves a three-step process: Research for Facts, Review for Meaning, and Respond for Life.

4. Pray, if appropriate for your setting and the people involved.

STEP ONE: RESEARCH FOR FACTS
(allow 15 minutes)

1. Explain that the goal of Step One is to find answers to the fact-finding questions in the left margin in order to establish the foundation for discovering meanings in Step Two.

2. Invite people to read through the passage on their own, looking for significant facts of the story. Discoveries may be written in the left margin, circled, or underlined. Answers may not be found for all questions.

3. After 5-7 minutes of personal study, begin the discussion by asking, "What did you discover about who is involved and what is happening? What did you discover regarding how people are responding?"

4. Move to Step Two after 8-10 minutes of discussion even if all facts are not yet discussed.

STEP TWO: REVIEW FOR MEANING
(allow 25 minutes)

1. Explain that the goal of Step Two is to discover meanings by making observations about the passage using the five analysis questions in the right margin.

2. Invite people to reread the passage, making their own personal observations and responses to the five questions. Again, they may write in the margin, underline, circle or highlight with different colored pens. Answers may not be found for all questions.

3. After 7-9 minutes, begin the discussion by asking, "What repetition, contrast, or comparison did you observe? Why are these important to the meaning of the passage for you?"

28

4. For additional discussion and discovery of meaning, choose from the following questions:

    ◢ What do you discover about God in this passage? Why do you think this is significant?

    ◢ How would you describe Mary's relationship with God?

    ◢ What do you discover about her responses to God's messenger? How do they change? Why do you think her responses change?

    ◢ In what way does this passage answer the question, "How is Jesus unique?" Why is this significant for today or for you personally?

5. After 15 minutes of discussion, affirm the value of all observations shared and move to explain Step Three.

STEP THREE: RESPOND FOR LIFE   (allow 10 minutes)

1. Explain that the goal of Step Three is to reflect on personal meanings or biblical insights discovered and to ponder possible responses for our personal lives.

2. Choose one of the following options that seems most appropriate for the people, the setting, or the observations shared. People may share responses with each other, write reflections in the bottom margin, or ponder privately.

    Option One. Invite people to reflect on their personal responses to the meanings of this passage. You may review the responses in the bottom margin under Respond for Life to stimulate their reflection.

    Option Two. Select one of the following questions to assist people in their reflection on or response to personal meanings or biblical insights from this passage:

    ◢ Consider Mary's response to God's message and what it may cost her. In what way is her response similar to and/or different from your own response to God? How is Mary an example for you? What do you find most difficult about her response to God, and why?

    ◢ What do you find significant about the angel's message that Jesus will be holy and his birth supernatural? How is this unique?

TO CLOSE   (allow 5 minutes)

1. Pray—privately, together, or not at all—as appropriate for the setting and the people involved.

2. Agree on time, place, and discussion leader for the next conversational Bible study.

FUTURE STUDY LIST

A UNIQUE BEGINNING
Luke 1:26-38

30-MINUTE DISCUSSION GUIDE

TO BEGIN (allow 5 minutes)

1. Look at the Bible Study and Background Information sheet for Luke 1:26-38.

2. Read the Background Information, then review the Discussion Guidelines with everyone.

3. Explain that the study/discussion involves a three-step process: Research for Facts, Review for Meaning, and Respond for Life.

4. Pray, if appropriate for your setting and the people involved.

STEP ONE: RESEARCH FOR FACTS (allow 6-7 minutes)

1. Explain that since there is limited time, the goal of Step One is to find answers to just the first three questions in the left margin in order to establish the foundation for discovering meanings in Step Two.

2. Read the passage aloud, then invite people to review it on their own, looking for significant facts of the story. Discoveries may be written in the left margin, circled, or underlined. Answers may not be found for all questions.

3. After 3-4 minutes of personal study, begin the discussion by asking, "What did you discover about who is involved and what is happening? What did you discover regarding how people are responding?"

4. Move to Step Two after 3-4 minutes of discussion even if all facts are not yet discussed.

STEP TWO: REVIEW FOR MEANING (allow 10-12 minutes)

1. Explain that the goal of Step Two is to discover meanings by making observations about the passage using the first three analysis questions in the right margin.

2. Invite people to reread the passage, making their own personal observations and responses to the first three questions. Again they may write in the margin, underline, circle or highlight with different colored pens. Answers may not be found for all questions.

3. After 5-6 minutes, begin the discussion by asking, "What repetition, contrast, or comparison did you observe? Why are these important to the meaning of the passage for you?"

4.　For additional discussion and discovery of meaning, choose from the following questions:

　　🔰 How would you describe Mary's relationship with God?

　　🔰 Why do you think her responses to God's messenger change during the conversation?

　　🔰 In what way does this passage answer the question, "How is Jesus unique?" Why is this significant for today or for you personally?

5.　After 5-6 minutes of discussion, affirm the value of all observations shared and move to explain Step Three.

STEP THREE: RESPOND FOR LIFE　　　　　　　　　　　　　　　　(allow 5 minutes)

1.　Explain that the goal of Step Three is to reflect on personal meanings or biblical insights discovered and to ponder possible responses for our personal lives.

2.　Choose one of the following options that seems most appropriate for the people, the setting, or the observations shared. People may share responses with each other, write reflections in the bottom margin, or ponder privately.

　　Option One. Invite people to reflect on their personal responses to the meanings of this passage. You may review the responses in the bottom margin under Respond for Life to stimulate their reflection.

　　Option Two. Select one of the following questions to assist people in their reflection on or response to personal meanings or biblical insights from this passage:

　　🔰 Consider Mary's response to God's message and what it may cost her. In what way is her response similar to and/or different from your own response to God? How is Mary an example for you? What do you find most difficult about her response to God, and why?

　　🔰 What do you find significant about the angel's message that Jesus will be holy and his birth supernatural? How is this unique?

TO CLOSE　　　　　　　　　　　　　　　　　　　　　　　　　(allow 5 minutes)

1.　Pray—privately, together, or not at all—as appropriate for the setting and the people involved.

2.　Agree on time, place, and discussion leader for the next conversational Bible study.

FUTURE STUDY LIST

WHO CALMS THE SEA?
Mark 4:35-41

60-MINUTE DISCUSSION GUIDE

TO BEGIN (allow 5 minutes)

1. Look at the Bible Study and Background Information sheet for Mark 4:35-41.

2. Read the Background Information, then review the Discussion Guidelines with everyone.

3. Explain that the study/discussion involves a three-step process: Research for Facts, Review for Meaning, and Respond for Life.

4. Pray, if appropriate for your setting and the people involved.

STEP ONE: **RESEARCH FOR FACTS** (allow 15 minutes)

1. Explain that the goal of Step One is to find answers to the fact-finding questions in the left margin in order to establish the foundation for discovering meanings in Step Two.

2. Invite people to read through the passage on their own, looking for significant facts of the story. Discoveries may be written in the left margin, circled, or underlined. Answers may not be found for all questions.

3. After 5-7 minutes of personal study, begin the discussion by asking, "What did you discover about who is involved and what is happening? What did you discover regarding how people are responding?"

4. Move to Step Two after 8-10 minutes of discussion even if all facts are not yet discussed.

STEP TWO: **REVIEW FOR MEANING** (allow 25 minutes)

1. Explain that the goal of Step Two is to discover meanings by making observations about the passage using the five analysis questions in the right margin.

2. Invite people to reread the passage, making their own personal observations and responses to the five questions. Again, they may write in the margin, underline, circle or highlight with different colored pens. Answers may not be found for all questions.

3. After 7-9 minutes, begin the discussion by asking, "What repetition, contrast, or comparison did you observe? Why are these important to the meaning of the passage for you?

4. For additional discussion and discovery of meaning, choose from the following questions:

    ◿ What does this event reveal about Jesus?

    ◿ In what ways does Jesus' behavior surprise you? How did it surprise the disciples?

    ◿ What emotions do you think the disciples experienced? Do you think the disciples expected that Jesus could rescue them? Why or why not?

    ◿ Why do you think Jesus seemed surprised that the disciples were afraid? What did he expect of them?

    ◿ What does the word "faith" seem to mean in this story?

    ◿ Why do you think the disciples raised the question, "Who then is this, that even the wind and the sea obey him"?

    ◿ How do you think this experience affected the disciples?

5. After 15 minutes of discussion, affirm the value of all observations shared and move to explain Step Three.

STEP THREE: **RESPOND FOR LIFE**   (allow 10 minutes)

1. Explain that the goal of Step Three is to reflect on personal meanings or biblical insights discovered and to ponder possible reponses for our personal lives.

2. Choose one of the following options that seems most appropriate for the people, the setting, or the observations shared. People may share responses with each other, write reflections in the bottom margin, or ponder privately.

    Option One. Invite people to reflect on their personal responses to the meanings of this passage. You may review the responses in the bottom margin under Respond for Life to stimulate their reflection.

    Option Two. Select one of the following questions to assist people in their reflection on or response to personal meanings or biblical insights from this passage:

    ◿ If you had been one of the disciples, how would this experience have affected you? Why?

    ◿ The disciples incorrectly assumed Jesus didn't care about them. What makes you question whether Jesus cares for you? How can you discover his care for you?

TO CLOSE   (allow 5 minutes)

1. Pray—privately, together, or not at all—as appropriate for the setting and the people involved.

2. Agree on time, place, and discussion leader for the next conversational Bible study.

FUTURE STUDY LIST

WHO CALMS THE SEA?
Mark 4:35-41
⬇

30-MINUTE DISCUSSION GUIDE

TO BEGIN   (allow 5 minutes)

1. Look at the Bible Study and Background Information sheet for Mark 4:35-41.

2. Read the Background Information, then review the Discussion Guidelines with everyone.

3. Explain that the study/discussion involves a three-step process: Research for Facts, Review for Meaning, and Respond for Life.

4. Pray, if appropriate for your setting and the people involved.

STEP ONE: RESEARCH FOR FACTS   (allow 6-7 minutes)

1. Explain that since there is limited time, the goal of Step One is to find answers to just the first three questions in the left margin in order to establish the foundation for discovering meanings in Step Two.

2. Read the passage aloud, then invite people to review it on their own, looking for significant facts of the story. Discoveries may be written in the left margin, circled, or underlined. Answers may not be found for all questions.

3. After 3-4 minutes of personal study, begin the discussion by asking, "What did you discover about who is involved and what is happening? What did you discover regarding how people are responding?"

4. Move to Step Two after 3-4 minutes of discussion even if all facts are not yet discussed.

STEP TWO: REVIEW FOR MEANING   (allow 10-12 minutes)

1. Explain that the goal of Step Two is to discover meanings by making observations about the passage using the first three analysis questions in the right margin.

2. Invite people to reread the passage, making their own personal observations and responses to the first three questions. Again they may write in the margin, underline, circle or highlight with different colored pens. Answers may not be found for all questions.

3. After 5-6 minutes, begin the discussion by asking, "What repetition, contrast, or comparison did you observe? Why are these important to the meaning of the passage for you?

34

4. For additional discussion and discovery of meaning, choose from the following questions:

 ◢ In what ways does Jesus' behavior surprise you? How did it surprise the disciples?

 ◢ What emotions do you think the disciples experienced? Do you think the disciples expected that Jesus could rescue them? Why or why not?

 ◢ What does the word "faith" seem to mean in this story?

 ◢ Why do you think the disciples raised the question, "Who then is this, that even the wind and the sea obey him"?

5. After 5-6 minutes of discussion, affirm the value of all observations shared and move to explain Step Three.

STEP THREE: RESPOND FOR LIFE   (allow 5 minutes)

1. Explain that the goal of Step Three is to reflect on personal meanings or biblical insights discovered and to ponder possible responses for our personal lives.

2. Choose one of the following options that seems most appropriate for the people, the setting, or the observations shared. People may share responses with each other, write reflections in the bottom margin, or ponder privately.

 Option One. Invite people to reflect on their personal responses to the meanings of this passage. You may review the responses in the bottom margin under Respond for Life to stimulate their reflection.

 Option Two. Select one of the following questions to assist people in their reflection on or response to personal meanings or biblical insights from this passage:

 ◢ If you had been one of the disciples, how would this experience have affected you? Why?

 ◢ The disciples incorrectly assumed Jesus didn't care about them. What makes you question whether Jesus cares for you? How might you begin to discover his care for you?

TO CLOSE   (allow 5 minutes)

1. Pray—privately, together, or not at all—as appropriate for the setting and the people involved.

2. Agree on time, place, and discussion leader for the next conversational Bible study.

FUTURE STUDY LIST

WHO CAN FORGIVE?
Mark 2:1-12

To Begin   (allow 5 minutes)

1. Look at the Bible Study and Background Information sheet for Mark 2:1-12.

2. Read the Background Information, then review the Discussion Guidelines with everyone.

3. Explain that the study/discussion involves a three-step process: Research for Facts, Review for Meaning, and Respond for Life.

4. Pray, if appropriate for your setting and the people involved.

Step One: RESEARCH FOR FACTS   (allow 15 minutes)

1. Explain that the goal of Step One is to find answers to the fact-finding questions in the left margin in order to establish the foundation for discovering meanings in Step Two.

2. Invite people to read through the passage on their own, looking for significant facts of the story. Discoveries may be written in the left margin, circled, or underlined. Answers may not be found for all questions.

3. After 5-7 minutes of personal study, begin the discussion by asking, "What did you discover about who is involved and what is happening? What did you discover regarding how people are responding?"

4. Move to Step Two after 8-10 minutes of discussion even if all facts are not yet discussed.

Step Two: REVIEW FOR MEANING   (allow 25 minutes)

1. Explain that the goal of Step Two is to discover meanings by making observations about the passage using the five analysis questions in the right margin.

2. Invite people to reread the passage, making their own personal observations and responses to the five questions. Again, they may write in the margin, underline, circle or highlight with different colored pens. Answers may not be found for all questions.

3. After 7-9 minutes, begin the discussion by asking, "What repetition, contrast, or comparison did you observe? Why are these important to the meaning of the passage for you?

4. For additional discussion and discovery of meaning, choose from the following questions:

   - What does this event suggest about the paralyzed man's friends? What did they expect from Jesus? What did they risk by their unorthodox behavior?

   - What do you discover about Jesus in this passage? What is most significant about what Jesus said or did? Why?

   - What did Jesus hope to communicate to the people? What was he most concerned about?

   - How were the various people in this story affected by Jesus' actions? Why do you think each of them responded as they did?

5. After 15 minutes of discussion, affirm the value of all observations shared and move to explain Step Three.

STEP THREE: RESPOND FOR LIFE   (allow 10 minutes)

1. Explain that the goal of Step Three is to reflect on personal meanings or biblical insights discovered and to ponder possible responses for our personal lives.

2. Choose one of the following options that seems most appropriate for the people, the setting, or the observations shared. People may share responses with each other, write reflections in the bottom margin, or ponder privately.

   Option One. Invite people to reflect on their personal responses to the meanings of this passage. You may review the responses in the bottom margin under Respond for Life to stimulate their reflection.

   Option Two. Select one of the following questions to assist people in their reflection on or response to personal meanings or biblical insights from this passage:

   - Imagine yourself as a part of this event. How would you have been affected? Would you have responded more like the people in verse 12, or like the religious leaders in verse 7? Why?

   - Picture yourself as the paralyzed man. What do you desire Jesus to do for you? Why is experiencing the forgiveness of sin a great need? How might this forgiveness change you?

TO CLOSE   (allow 5 minutes)

1. Pray—privately, together, or not at all—as appropriate for the setting and the people involved.

2. Agree on time, place, and discussion leader for the next conversational Bible study.

FUTURE STUDY LIST

WHO CAN FORGIVE?
Mark 2:1-12
⬇

30-MINUTE DISCUSSION GUIDE

TO BEGIN (allow 5 minutes)

1. Look at the Bible Study and Background Information sheet for Mark 2:1-12.

2. Read the Background Information, then review the Discussion Guidelines with everyone.

3. Explain that the study/discussion involves a three-step process: Research for Facts, Review for Meaning, and Respond for Life.

4. Pray, if appropriate for your setting and the people involved.

STEP ONE: RESEARCH FOR FACTS (allow 6-7 minutes)

1. Explain that since there is limited time, the goal of Step One is to find answers to just the first three questions in the left margin in order to establish the foundation for discovering meanings in Step Two.

2. Read the passage aloud, then invite people to review it on their own, looking for significant facts of the story. Discoveries may be written in the left margin, circled, or underlined. Answers may not be found for all questions.

3. After 3-4 minutes of personal study, begin the discussion by asking, "What did you discover about who is involved and what is happening? What did you discover regarding how people are responding?"

4. Move to Step Two after 3-4 minutes of discussion even if all facts are not yet discussed.

STEP TWO: REVIEW FOR MEANING (allow 10-12 minutes)

1. Explain that the goal of Step Two is to discover meanings by making observations about the passage using the first three analysis questions in the right margin.

2. Invite people to reread the passage, making their own personal observations and responses to the first three questions. Again they may write in the margin, underline, circle or highlight with different colored pens. Answers may not be found for all questions.

3. After 5-6 minutes, begin the discussion by asking, "What repetition, contrast, or comparison did you observe? Why are these important to the meaning of the passage for you?

4. For additional discussion and discovery of meaning, choose from the following questions:

    ◤ What does this event suggest about the paralyzed man's friends? What did they expect from Jesus? What did they risk by their unorthodox behavior?

    ◤ What do you discover about Jesus in this passage? What is most significant about what Jesus said or did? Why?

    ◤ How were the various people in this story affected by Jesus' actions? Why do you think each of them responded as they did?

5. After 5-6 minutes of discussion, affirm the value of all observations shared and move to explain Step Three.

STEP THREE: RESPOND FOR LIFE   (allow 5 minutes)

1. Explain that the goal of Step Three is to reflect on personal meanings or biblical insights discovered and to ponder possible responses for our personal lives.

2. Choose one of the following options that seems most appropriate for the people, the setting, or the observations shared. People may share responses with each other, write reflections in the bottom margin, or ponder privately.

    Option One. Invite people to reflect on their personal responses to the meanings of this passage. You may review the responses in the bottom margin under Respond for Life to stimulate their reflection.

    Option Two. Select one of the following questions to assist people in their reflection on or response to personal meanings or biblical insights from this passage:

    ◤ Imagine yourself as a part of this event. How would you have been affected? Would you have responded more like the people in verse 12, or like the religious leaders in verse 7? Why?

    ◤ Picture yourself as the paralyzed man. What do you desire Jesus to do for you? Why is experiencing the forgiveness of sin a great need? How might this forgiveness change you?

TO CLOSE   (allow 5 minutes)

1. Pray—privately, together, or not at all—as appropriate for the setting and the people involved.

2. Agree on time, place, and discussion leader for the next conversational Bible study.

FUTURE STUDY LIST

WHO COMMANDS THE SPIRITS?
Mark 9:14-27

To Begin (allow 5 minutes)

1. Look at the Bible Study and Background Information sheet for Mark 9:14-27.

2. Read the Background Information, then review the Discussion Guidelines with everyone.

3. Explain that the study/discussion involves a three-step process: Research for Facts, Review for Meaning, and Respond for Life.

4. Pray, if appropriate for your setting and the people involved.

Step One: RESEARCH FOR FACTS (allow 15 minutes)

1. Explain that the goal of Step One is to find answers to the fact-finding questions in the left margin in order to establish the foundation for discovering meanings in Step Two.

2. Invite people to read through the passage on their own, looking for significant facts of the story. Discoveries may be written in the left margin, circled, or underlined. Answers may not be found for all questions.

3. After 5-7 minutes of personal study, begin the discussion by asking, "What did you discover about who is involved and what is happening? What did you discover regarding how people are responding?"

4. Move to Step Two after 8-10 minutes of discussion even if all facts are not yet discussed.

Step Two: REVIEW FOR MEANING (allow 25 minutes)

1. Explain that the goal of Step Two is to discover meanings by making observations about the passage using the five analysis questions in the right margin.

2. Invite people to reread the passage, making their own personal observations and responses to the five questions. Again, they may write in the margin, underline, circle or highlight with different colored pens. Answers may not be found for all questions.

3. After 7-9 minutes, begin the discussion by asking, "What repetition, contrast, or comparison did you observe? Why are these important to the meaning of the passage for you?

4. For additional discussion and discovery of meaning, choose from the following questions:

    ◢ What do you discover about Jesus? What surprises you, and why?

    ◢ What do you notice regarding the contrast between Jesus and the demonic spirit? How are they different? Why is this significant?

    ◢ How would you describe the father's experience in this passage?

    ◢ Why was Jesus deeply troubled with the disciples? What did he desire for them?

    ◢ How does Jesus respond to the father's cry, "Help my unbelief"? Do you think it helped his unbelief? Why or why not?

5. After 15 minutes of discussion, affirm the value of all observations shared and move to explain Step Three.

STEP THREE: RESPOND FOR LIFE   (allow 10 minutes)

1. Explain that the goal of Step Three is to reflect on personal meanings or biblical insights discovered and to ponder possible responses for our personal lives.

2. Choose one of the following options that seems most appropriate for the people, the setting, or the observations shared. People may share responses with each other, write reflections in the bottom margin, or ponder privately.

    Option One. Invite people to reflect on their personal responses to the meanings of this passage. You may review the responses in the bottom margin under Respond for Life to stimulate their reflection.

    Option Two. Select one of the following questions to assist people in their reflection on or response to personal meanings or biblical insights from this passage:

    ◢ As you look at Jesus in this passage, what is most significant to you, and why?

    ◢ In what way can you identify with the father's struggle to believe Jesus can heal his son? What are you struggling to believe about Jesus?

TO CLOSE   (allow 5 minutes)

1. Pray—privately, together, or not at all—as appropriate for the setting and the people involved.

2. Agree on time, place, and discussion leader for the next conversational Bible study.

FUTURE STUDY LIST

WHO COMMANDS THE SPIRITS?
Mark 9:14-27
🔻

30-MINUTE DISCUSSION GUIDE

TO BEGIN   (allow 5 minutes)

1. Look at the Bible Study and Background Information sheet for Mark 9:14-27.

2. Read the Background Information, then review the Discussion Guidelines with everyone.

3. Explain that the study/discussion involves a three-step process: Research for Facts, Review for Meaning, and Respond for Life.

4. Pray, if appropriate for your setting and the people involved.

STEP ONE: RESEARCH FOR FACTS   (allow 6-7 minutes)

1. Explain that since there is limited time, the goal of Step One is to find answers to just the first three questions in the left margin in order to establish the foundation for discovering meanings in Step Two.

2. Read the passage aloud, then invite people to review it on their own, looking for significant facts of the story. Discoveries may be written in the left margin, circled, or underlined. Answers may not be found for all questions.

3. After 3-4 minutes of personal study, begin the discussion by asking, "What did you discover about who is involved and what is happening? What did you discover regarding how people are responding?"

4. Move to Step Two after 3-4 minutes of discussion even if all facts are not yet discussed.

STEP TWO: REVIEW FOR MEANING   (allow 10-12 minutes)

1. Explain that the goal of Step Two is to discover meanings by making observations about the passage using the first three analysis questions in the right margin.

2. Invite people to reread the passage, making their own personal observations and responses to the first three questions. Again they may write in the margin, underline, circle or highlight with different colored pens. Answers may not be found for all questions.

3. After 5-6 minutes, begin the discussion by asking, "What repetition, contrast, or comparison did you observe? Why are these important to the meaning of the passage for you?

4. For additional discussion and discovery of meaning, choose from the following questions:

   ◥ What do you discover about Jesus? What surprises you, and why?

   ◥ What do you notice regarding the contrast between Jesus and the demonic spirit? How are they different? Why is this significant?

   ◥ How would you describe the father's experience in this passage?

   ◥ Why was Jesus deeply troubled with the disciples? What did he desire for them?

5. After 5-6 minutes of discussion, affirm the value of all observations shared and move to explain Step Three.

STEP THREE: RESPOND FOR LIFE   (allow 5 minutes)

1. Explain that the goal of Step Three is to reflect on personal meanings or biblical insights discovered and to ponder possible responses for our personal lives.

2. Choose one of the following options that seems most appropriate for the people, the setting, or the observations shared. People may share responses with each other, write reflections in the bottom margin, or ponder privately.

   Option One. Invite people to reflect on their personal responses to the meanings of this passage. You may review the responses in the bottom margin under Respond for Life to stimulate their reflection.

   Option Two. Select one of the following questions to assist people in their reflection on or response to personal meanings or biblical insights from this passage:

   ◥ As you look at Jesus in this passage, what is most significant to you, and why?

   ◥ In what way can you identify with the father's struggle to believe Jesus can heal his son? What are you struggling to believe about Jesus?

TO CLOSE   (allow 5 minutes)

1. Pray—privately, together, or not at all—as appropriate for the setting and the people involved.

2. Agree on time, place, and discussion leader for the next conversational Bible study.

FUTURE STUDY LIST

WHO RAISES THE DEAD?
Luke 7:11-17

60-MINUTE DISCUSSION GUIDE

TO BEGIN (allow 5 minutes)

1. Look at the Bible Study and Background Information sheet for Luke 7:11-17.

2. Read the Background Information, then review the Discussion Guidelines with everyone.

3. Explain that the study/discussion involves a three-step process: Research for Facts, Review for Meaning, and Respond for Life.

4. Pray, if appropriate for your setting and the people involved.

STEP ONE: RESEARCH FOR FACTS (allow 15 minutes)

1. Explain that the goal of Step One is to find answers to the fact-finding questions in the left margin in order to establish the foundation for discovering meanings in Step Two.

2. Invite people to read through the passage on their own, looking for significant facts of the story. Discoveries may be written in the left margin, circled, or underlined. Answers may not be found for all questions.

3. After 5-7 minutes of personal study, begin the discussion by asking, "What did you discover about who is involved and what is happening? What did you discover regarding how people are responding?"

4. Move to Step Two after 8-10 minutes of discussion even if all facts are not yet discussed.

STEP TWO: REVIEW FOR MEANING (allow 25 minutes)

1. Explain that the goal of Step Two is to discover meanings by making observations about the passage using the five analysis questions in the right margin.

2. Invite people to reread the passage, making their own personal observations and responses to the five questions. Again, they may write in the margin, underline, circle or highlight with different colored pens. Answers may not be found for all questions.

3. After 7-9 minutes, begin the discussion by asking, "What repetition, contrast, or comparison did you observe? Why are these important to the meaning of the passage for you?

4. For additional discussion and discovery of meaning, choose from the following questions:

    ◢ What do you discover about Jesus in this passage? What do you find attractive, and why?

    ◢ Why does Jesus raise the young man to life? What does this indicate about Jesus?

    ◢ Why do you think the crowd praises God? What does this suggest about Jesus?

    ◢ Why does Jesus break the Jewish rules of his day? What might this suggest about Jesus?

5. After 15 minutes of discussion, affirm the value of all observations shared and move to explain Step Three.

STEP THREE: **RESPOND FOR LIFE**   (allow 10 minutes)

1. Explain that the goal of Step Three is to reflect on personal meanings or biblical insights discovered and to ponder possible responses for our personal lives.

2. Choose one of the following options that seems most appropriate for the people, the setting, or the observations shared. People may share responses with each other, write reflections in the bottom margin, or ponder privately.

    Option One. Invite people to reflect on their personal responses to the meanings of this passage. You may review the responses in the bottom margin under Respond for Life to stimulate their reflection.

    Option Two. Select one of the following questions to assist people in their reflection on or response to personal meanings or biblical insights from this passage:

    ◢ If you had been the widow, how would this encounter have changed your view of Jesus? How do you wish Jesus would touch your life today?

    ◢ What could Jesus do that would demonstrate his compassion for you? Consider inviting him through prayer to do that now.

TO CLOSE   (allow 5 minutes)

1. Pray—privately, together, or not at all—as appropriate for the setting and the people involved.

2. Agree on time, place, and discussion leader for the next conversational Bible study.

FUTURE STUDY LIST

WHO RAISES THE DEAD?
Luke 7:11-17
⬇

30-MINUTE DISCUSSION GUIDE

TO BEGIN (allow 5 minutes)

1. Look at the Bible Study and Background Information sheet for Luke 7:11-17.

2. Read the Background Information, then review the Discussion Guidelines with everyone.

3. Explain that the study/discussion involves a three-step process: Research for Facts, Review for Meaning, and Respond for Life.

4. Pray, if appropriate for your setting and the people involved.

STEP ONE: RESEARCH FOR FACTS (allow 6-7 minutes)

1. Explain that since there is limited time, the goal of Step One is to find answers to just the first three questions in the left margin in order to establish the foundation for discovering meanings in Step Two.

2. Read the passage aloud, then invite people to review it on their own, looking for significant facts of the story. Discoveries may be written in the left margin, circled, or underlined. Answers may not be found for all questions.

3. After 3-4 minutes of personal study, begin the discussion by asking, "What did you discover about who is involved and what is happening? What did you discover regarding how people are responding?"

4. Move to Step Two after 3-4 minutes of discussion even if all facts are not yet discussed.

STEP TWO: REVIEW FOR MEANING (allow 10-12 minutes)

1. Explain that the goal of Step Two is to discover meanings by making observations about the passage using the first three analysis questions in the right margin.

2. Invite people to reread the passage, making their own personal observations and responses to the first three questions. Again they may write in the margin, underline, circle or highlight with different colored pens. Answers may not be found for all questions.

3. After 5-6 minutes, begin the discussion by asking, "What repetition, contrast, or comparison did you observe? Why are these important to the meaning of the passage for you?

4. For additional discussion and discovery of meaning, choose from the following questions:

    ⬨ What do you discover about Jesus in this passage? What do you find attractive, and why?

    ⬨ Why does Jesus raise the young man to life? What does this indicate about Jesus?

    ⬨ Why do you think the crowd praises God? What does this suggest about Jesus?

5. After 5-6 minutes of discussion, affirm the value of all observations shared and move to explain Step Three.

STEP THREE: RESPOND FOR LIFE   (allow 5 minutes)

1. Explain that the goal of Step Three is to reflect on personal meanings or biblical insights discovered and to ponder possible responses for our personal lives.

2. Choose one of the following options that seems most appropriate for the people, the setting, or the observations shared. People may share responses with each other, write reflections in the bottom margin, or ponder privately.

    Option One. Invite people to reflect on their personal responses to the meanings of this passage. You may review the responses in the bottom margin under Respond for Life to stimulate their reflection.

    Option Two. Select one of the following questions to assist people in their reflection on or response to personal meanings or biblical insights from this passage:

    ⬨ If you had been the widow, how would this encounter have changed your view of Jesus? How do you wish Jesus would touch your life today?

    ⬨ What could Jesus do that would demonstrate his compassion for you? Consider inviting him through prayer to do that now.

TO CLOSE   (allow 5 minutes)

1. Pray—privately, together, or not at all—as appropriate for the setting and the people involved.

2. Agree on time, place, and discussion leader for the next conversational Bible study.

FUTURE STUDY LIST

WHO WILL NEVER DIE?
John 11:20-44

60-MINUTE DISCUSSION GUIDE

TO BEGIN   (allow 5 minutes)

1. Look at the Bible Study and Background Information sheet for John 11:20-44.

2. Read the Background Information, then review the Discussion Guidelines with everyone.

3. Explain that the study/discussion involves a three-step process: Research for Facts, Review for Meaning, and Respond for Life.

4. Pray, if appropriate for your setting and the people involved.

STEP ONE: RESEARCH FOR FACTS   (allow 15 minutes)

1. Explain that the goal of Step One is to find answers to the fact-finding questions in the left margin in order to establish the foundation for discovering meanings in Step Two.

2. Invite people to read through the passage on their own, looking for significant facts of the story. Discoveries may be written in the left margin, circled, or underlined. Answers may not be found for all questions.

3. After 5-7 minutes of personal study, begin the discussion by asking, "What did you discover about who is involved and what is happening? What did you discover regarding how people are responding?"

4. Move to Step Two after 8-10 minutes of discussion even if all facts are not yet discussed.

STEP TWO: REVIEW FOR MEANING   (allow 25 minutes)

1. Explain that the goal of Step Two is to discover meanings by making observations about the passage using the five analysis questions in the right margin.

2. Invite people to reread the passage, making their own personal observations and responses to the five questions. Again, they may write in the margin, underline, circle or highlight with different colored pens. Answers may not be found for all questions.

3. After 7-9 minutes, begin the discussion by asking, "What repetition, contrast, or comparison did you observe? Why are these important to the meaning of the passage for you?

4. For additional discussion and discovery of meaning, choose from the following questions:

    ❧ What do you discover about Jesus in this passage? What does he want people to believe about him? Why is that important?

    ❧ What did Mary and Martha believe Jesus could do and not do for their brother? How did Jesus go beyond their expectation? Why is this significant?

    ❧ What does this whole event demonstrate about Jesus and his concerns? What do you find most surprising? Why?

    ❧ What does Jesus state about himself? What does he promise? Why do you think this is significant?

    ❧ From this passage, why is Jesus unique?

5. After 15 minutes of discussion, affirm the value of all observations shared and move to explain Step Three.

STEP THREE: **RESPOND FOR LIFE**　　　　　　　　　　　　　　　　　　　(allow 10 minutes)

1. Explain that the goal of Step Three is to reflect on personal meanings or biblical insights discovered and to ponder possible responses for our personal lives.

2. Choose one of the following options that seems most appropriate for the people, the setting, or the observations shared. People may share responses with each other, write reflections in the bottom margin, or ponder privately.

    Option One. Invite people to reflect on their personal responses to the meanings of this passage. You may review the responses in the bottom margin under Respond for Life to stimulate their reflection.

    Option Two. Select one of the following questions to assist people in their reflection on or response to personal meanings or biblical insights from this passage:

    ❧ Put yourself in Mary and Martha's place. If Jesus brought your dead brother back to life, how would you react? How might it change what you believe about Jesus?

    ❧ Consider Jesus' offer for those who believe in him. How would this offer change your life if you accepted it today?

TO CLOSE　　　　　　　　　　　　　　　　　　　　　　　　　　　　　(allow 5 minutes)

1. Pray—privately, together, or not at all—as appropriate for the setting and the people involved.

2. Agree on time, place, and discussion leader for the next conversational Bible study.

FUTURE STUDY LIST

49

WHO WILL NEVER DIE?
John 11:20-44
⬇

30-MINUTE DISCUSSION GUIDE

TO BEGIN (allow 5 minutes)

---

1. Look at the Bible Study and Background Information sheet for John 11:20-44.

2. Read the Background Information, then review the Discussion Guidelines with everyone.

3. Explain that the study/discussion involves a three-step process: Research for Facts, Review for Meaning, and Respond for Life.

4. Pray, if appropriate for your setting and the people involved.

STEP ONE: RESEARCH FOR FACTS (allow 6-7 minutes)

---

1. Explain that since there is limited time, the goal of Step One is to find answers to just the first three questions in the left margin in order to establish the foundation for discovering meanings in Step Two.

2. Read the passage aloud, then invite people to review it on their own, looking for significant facts of the story. Discoveries may be written in the left margin, circled, or underlined. Answers may not be found for all questions.

3. After 3-4 minutes of personal study, begin the discussion by asking, "What did you discover about who is involved and what is happening? What did you discover regarding how people are responding?"

4. Move to Step Two after 3-4 minutes of discussion even if all facts are not yet discussed.

STEP TWO: REVIEW FOR MEANING (allow 10-12 minutes)

---

1. Explain that the goal of Step Two is to discover meanings by making observations about the passage using the first three analysis questions in the right margin.

2. Invite people to reread the passage, making their own personal observations and responses to the first three questions. Again they may write in the margin, underline, circle or highlight with different colored pens. Answers may not be found for all questions.

3. After 5-6 minutes, begin the discussion by asking, "What repetition, contrast, or comparison did you observe? Why are these important to the meaning of the passage for you?

4. For additional discussion and discovery of meaning, choose from the following questions:

    🔊 What do you discover about Jesus in this passage? What does he want people to believe about him? Why is that important?

    🔊 What did Mary and Martha believe Jesus could do and not do for their brother? How did Jesus go beyond their expectation? Why is this significant?

    🔊 What does Jesus state about himself? What does he promise? Why do you think this is significant?

5. After 5-6 minutes of discussion, affirm the value of all observations shared and move to explain Step Three.

STEP THREE: RESPOND FOR LIFE   (allow 5 minutes)

1. Explain that the goal of Step Three is to reflect on personal meanings or biblical insights discovered and to ponder possible responses for our personal lives.

2. Choose one of the following options that seems most appropriate for the people, the setting, or the observations shared. People may share responses with each other, write reflections in the bottom margin, or ponder privately.

    Option One. Invite people to reflect on their personal responses to the meanings of this passage. You may review the responses in the bottom margin under Respond for Life to stimulate their reflection.

    Option Two. Select one of the following questions to assist people in their reflection on or response to personal meanings or biblical insights from this passage:

    🔊 Put yourself in Mary and Martha's place. If Jesus brought your dead brother back to life, how would you react? How might it change what you believe about Jesus?

    🔊 Consider Jesus' offer for those who believe in him. How would this offer change your life if you accepted it today?

TO CLOSE   (allow 5 minutes)

1. Pray—privately, together, or not at all—as appropriate for the setting and the people involved.

2. Agree on time, place, and discussion leader for the next conversational Bible study.

FUTURE STUDY LIST

WHERE IS HE?
Matthew 28:1-15

60-MINUTE DISCUSSION GUIDE

TO BEGIN (allow 5 minutes)

1. Look at the Bible Study and Background Information sheet for Matthew 28:1-15.

2. Read the Background Information, then review the Discussion Guidelines with everyone.

3. Explain that the study/discussion involves a three-step process: Research for Facts, Review for Meaning, and Respond for Life.

4. Pray, if appropriate for your setting and the people involved.

STEP ONE: RESEARCH FOR FACTS (allow 15 minutes)

1. Explain that the goal of Step One is to find answers to the fact-finding questions in the left margin in order to establish the foundation for discovering meanings in Step Two.

2. Invite people to read through the passage on their own, looking for significant facts of the story. Discoveries may be written in the left margin, circled, or underlined. Answers may not be found for all questions.

3. After 5-7 minutes of personal study, begin the discussion by asking, "What did you discover about who is involved and what is happening? What did you discover regarding how people are responding?"

4. Move to Step Two after 8-10 minutes of discussion even if all facts are not yet discussed.

STEP TWO: REVIEW FOR MEANING (allow 25 minutes)

1. Explain that the goal of Step Two is to discover meanings by making observations about the passage using the five analysis questions in the right margin.

2. Invite people to reread the passage, making their own personal observations and responses to the five questions. Again, they may write in the margin, underline, circle or highlight with different colored pens. Answers may not be found for all questions.

3. After 7-9 minutes, begin the discussion by asking, "What repetition, contrast, or comparison did you observe? Why are these important to the meaning of the passage for you?

4. For additional discussion and discovery of meaning, choose from the following questions:

    ⟍ What supernatural events are described? Why do people respond to them with fear?

    ⟍ Why were the women convinced that Jesus was alive?

    ⟍ How did the guards, the women, and the priests each respond to these events? Why did these people respond so differently?

    ⟍ When the women met Jesus, why do you think they responded in worship?

    ⟍ Why did the women respond to the angels so differently than the guards?

    ⟍ From this passage, how is Jesus unique?

5. After 15 minutes of discussion, affirm the value of all observations shared and move to explain Step Three.

STEP THREE: RESPOND FOR LIFE   (allow 10 minutes)

1. Explain that the goal of Step Three is to reflect on personal meanings or biblical insights discovered and to ponder possible responses for our personal lives.

2. Choose one of the following options that seems most appropriate for the people, the setting, or the observations shared. People may share responses with each other, write reflections in the bottom margin, or ponder privately.

    Option One. Invite people to reflect on their personal responses to the meanings of this passage. You may review the responses in the bottom margin under Respond for Life to stimulate their reflection.

    Option Two. Select one of the following questions to assist people in their reflection on or response to personal meanings or biblical insights from this passage:

    ⟍ If you were convinced that the resurrection of Jesus is real, how might it change your life? Why would it matter for you to believe that Jesus is alive today?

    ⟍ If people doubt that Jesus was raised from the dead, what evidence is there in this passage to help resolve their doubts? What doubts keep you from believing that Jesus is alive today?

TO CLOSE   (allow 5 minutes)

1. Pray—privately, together, or not at all—as appropriate for the setting and the people involved.

2. Agree on time, place, and discussion leader for the next conversational Bible study.

FUTURE STUDY LIST

WHERE IS HE?
Matthew 28:1-15

⬇

30-MINUTE DISCUSSION GUIDE

TO BEGIN (allow 5 minutes)

1. Look at the Bible Study and Background Information sheet for Matthew 28:1-15.

2. Read the Background Information, then review the Discussion Guidelines with everyone.

3. Explain that the study/discussion involves a three-step process: Research for Facts, Review for Meaning, and Respond for Life.

4. Pray, if appropriate for your setting and the people involved.

STEP ONE: RESEARCH FOR FACTS (allow 6-7 minutes)

1. Explain that since there is limited time, the goal of Step One is to find answers to just the first three questions in the left margin in order to establish the foundation for discovering meanings in Step Two.

2. Read the passage aloud, then invite people to review it on their own, looking for significant facts of the story. Discoveries may be written in the left margin, circled, or underlined. Answers may not be found for all questions.

4. Move to Step Two after 3-4 minutes of discussion even if all facts are not yet discussed.

STEP TWO: REVIEW FOR MEANING (allow 10-12 minutes)

1. Explain that the goal of Step Two is to discover meanings by making observations about the passage using the first three analysis questions in the right margin.

2. Invite people to reread the passage, making their own personal observations and responses to the first three questions. Again they may write in the margin, underline, circle or highlight with different colored pens. Answers may not be found for all questions.

3. After 5-6 minutes, begin the discussion by asking, "What repetition, contrast, or comparison did you observe? Why are these important to the meaning of the passage for you?

4. For additional discussion and discovery of meaning, choose from the following questions:

⬤ Why were the women convinced that Jesus was alive?

⬤ How did the guards, the women, and the priests each respond to these events? Why did these people react so differently?

⬤ When the women met Jesus, why do you think they responded in worship?

⬤ From this passage, why is Jesus unique?

5. After 5-6 minutes of discussion, affirm the value of all observations shared and move to explain Step Three.

STEP THREE: RESPOND FOR LIFE   (allow 5 minutes)

1. Explain that the goal of Step Three is to reflect on personal meanings or biblical insights discovered and to ponder possible responses for our personal lives.

2. Choose one of the following options that seems most appropriate for the people, the setting, or the observations shared. People may share responses with each other, write reflections in the bottom margin, or ponder privately.

Option One. Invite people to reflect on their personal responses to the meanings of this passage. You may review the responses in the bottom margin under Respond for Life to stimulate their reflection.

Option Two. Select one of the following questions to assist people in their reflection on or response to personal meanings or biblical insights from this passage:

⬤ If you were convinced that the resurrection of Jesus is real, how might it change your life? Why would it matter for you to believe that Jesus is alive today?

⬤ If people doubt that Jesus was raised from the dead, what evidence is there in this passage to help resolve their doubts? What doubts keep you from believing that Jesus is alive today?

TO CLOSE   (allow 5 minutes)

1. Pray—privately, together, or not at all—as appropriate for the setting and the people involved.

2. Agree on time, place, and discussion leader for the next conversational Bible study.

FUTURE STUDY LIST

I WILL NOT BELIEVE . . . UNLESS
John 20:24-31

TO BEGIN   (allow 5 minutes)

1. Look at the Bible Study and Background Information sheet for John 20:24-31.

2. Read the Background Information, then review the Discussion Guidelines with everyone.

3. Explain that the study/discussion involves a three-step process: Research for Facts, Review for Meaning, and Respond for Life.

4. Pray, if appropriate for your setting and the people involved.

STEP ONE: RESEARCH FOR FACTS   (allow 15 minutes)

1. Explain that the goal of Step One is to find answers to the fact-finding questions in the left margin in order to establish the foundation for discovering meanings in Step Two.

2. Invite people to read through the passage on their own, looking for significant facts of the story. Discoveries may be written in the left margin, circled, or underlined. Answers may not be found for all questions.

3. After 5-7 minutes of personal study, begin the discussion by asking, "What did you discover about who is involved and what is happening? What did you discover regarding how people are responding?"

4. Move to Step Two after 8-10 minutes of discussion even if all facts are not yet discussed.

STEP TWO: REVIEW FOR MEANING   (allow 25 minutes)

1. Explain that the goal of Step Two is to discover meanings by making observations about the passage using the five analysis questions in the right margin.

2. Invite people to reread the passage, making their own personal observations and responses to the five questions. Again, they may write in the margin, underline, circle or highlight with different colored pens. Answers may not be found for all questions.

3. After 7-9 minutes, begin the discussion by asking, "What repetition, contrast, or comparison did you observe? Why are these important to the meaning of the passage for you?

4. For additional discussion and discovery of meaning, choose from the following questions:

    ◢ What do you discover about Jesus in this passage? Why is that significant?

    ◢ Why do the disciples believe Jesus is alive? Why do they expect Thomas to believe?

    ◢ How does Jesus respond to Thomas? Why is this surprising? What does it suggest about Jesus' uniqueness?

    ◢ From Thomas' experience, what does he conclude about Jesus? Why does he make such a declaration?

    ◢ Why did the author write down these accounts of Jesus? What can one experience as a result of believing who Jesus is? Why is this significant?

5. After 15 minutes of discussion, affirm the value of all observations shared and move to explain Step Three.

STEP THREE: RESPOND FOR LIFE   (allow 10 minutes)

1. Explain that the goal of Step Three is to reflect on personal meanings or biblical insights discovered and to ponder possible responses for our personal lives.

2. Choose one of the following options that seems most appropriate for the people, the setting, or the observations shared. People may share responses with each other, write reflections in the bottom margin, or ponder privately.

    Option One. Invite people to reflect on their personal responses to the meanings of this passage. You may review the responses in the bottom margin under Respond for Life to stimulate their reflection.

    Option Two. Select one of the following questions to assist people in their reflection on or response to personal meanings or biblical insights from this passage:

    ◢ How does doubt affect your relationship with Jesus? What request would you make of Jesus that would help to dispel your doubt?

    ◢ Considering the meanings of "believe" and "Lord," if you were to respond to Jesus as Thomas did, "my Lord and my God," how would your daily life be different? How would it affect your work habits and relationships?

TO CLOSE   (allow 5 minutes)

1. Pray—privately, together, or not at all—as appropriate for the setting and the people involved.

2. Agree on time, place, and discussion leader for the next conversational Bible study.

FUTURE STUDY LIST

I WILL NOT BELIEVE . . . UNLESS
John 20:24-31
⬇

30-MINUTE DISCUSSION GUIDE

TO BEGIN   (allow 5 minutes)

1. Look at the Bible Study and Background Information sheet for John 20:24-31.

2. Read the Background Information, then review the Discussion Guidelines with everyone.

3. Explain that the study/discussion involves a three-step process: Research for Facts, Review for Meaning, and Respond for Life.

4. Pray, if appropriate for your setting and the people involved.

STEP ONE: RESEARCH FOR FACTS   (allow 6-7 minutes)

1. Explain that since there is limited time, the goal of Step One is to find answers to just the first three questions in the left margin in order to establish the foundation for discovering meanings in Step Two.

2. Read the passage aloud, then invite people to review it on their own, looking for significant facts of the story. Discoveries may be written in the left margin, circled, or underlined. Answers may not be found for all questions.

3. After 3-4 minutes of personal study, begin the discussion by asking, "What did you discover about who is involved and what is happening? What did you discover regarding how people are responding?"

4. Move to Step Two after 3-4 minutes of discussion even if all facts are not yet discussed.

STEP TWO: REVIEW FOR MEANING   (allow 10-12 minutes)

1. Explain that the goal of Step Two is to discover meanings by making observations about the passage using the first three analysis questions in the right margin.

2. Invite people to reread the passage, making their own personal observations and responses to the first three questions. Again they may write in the margin, underline, circle or highlight with different colored pens. Answers may not be found for all questions.

3. After 5-6 minutes, begin the discussion by asking, "What repetition, contrast, or comparison did you observe? Why are these important to the meaning of the passage for you?

4. For additional discussion and discovery of meaning, choose from the following questions:

    ⋟ What do you discover about Jesus in this passage? Why is that significant?

    ⋟ How does Jesus respond to Thomas? Why is this surprising? What does it suggest about Jesus' uniqueness?

    ⋟ From Thomas' experience, what does he conclude about Jesus? Why does he make such a declaration?

    ⋟ Why did the author write down these accounts of Jesus? What can one experience as a result of believing in Jesus? Why is this significant?

5. After 5-6 minutes of discussion, affirm the value of all observations shared and move to explain Step Three.

STEP THREE: **RESPOND FOR LIFE**   (allow 5 minutes)

1. Explain that the goal of Step Three is to reflect on personal meanings or biblical insights discovered and to ponder possible responses for our personal lives.

2. Choose one of the following options that seems most appropriate for the people, the setting, or the observations shared. People may share responses with each other, write reflections in the bottom margin, or ponder privately.

    Option One. Invite people to reflect on their personal responses to the meanings of this passage. You may review the responses in the bottom margin under Respond for Life to stimulate their reflection.

    Option Two. Select one of the following questions to assist people in their reflection on or response to personal meanings or biblical insights from this passage:

    ⋟ How does doubt affect your relationship with Jesus? What request would you make of Jesus that would help to dispel your doubt?

    ⋟ Considering the meaning of "believe" and "Lord," if you were to respond to Jesus as Thomas did, "my Lord and my God," how would your daily life be different? How would it affect your work habits and relationships?

TO CLOSE   (allow 5 minutes)

1. Pray—privately, together, or not at all—as appropriate for the setting and the people involved.

2. Agree on time, place, and discussion leader for the next conversational Bible study.

FUTURE STUDY LIST

Chapter Five
CONVERSATIONAL BIBLE STUDY AND BACKGROUND INFORMATION SHEETS

Luke 1:26-38
A UNIQUE BEGINNING

Background Information

Nazareth was an old and very small town in Galilee. Historical records suggest that the town was not highly thought of; it was relatively insignificant, and the Jews of Judea looked upon it with scorn.

The angel of the Lord comes to Mary in the sixth month of her relative Elizabeth's pregnancy. The announcement that Mary will give birth to a son shocks her. It likely carries with it public ridicule by her neighbors, who might assume she became pregnant by Joseph (or another man) during their engagement period. This was strictly forbidden in their culture.

This passage refers to numerous Old Testament passages that predicted how Jesus the Messiah would be born. The fact that Jesus would be a descendant of Israel's King David was very significant for the Jewish audience. Jesus, the long awaited Messiah, would be the everlasting King. He would come from the "house (or ancestral lineage) of David."

For Clarification

Mary was **betrothed**—engaged to be married—to Joseph. Engagement was legally binding, but the couple did not live together until after the wedding ceremony. Mary was uncertain of Joseph's response to her unprecedented pregnancy. Would he divorce her?

The **house of Jacob** is a traditional term to describe Israel.

To be addressed as **favored one** or **"you have found favor with God"** was a greeting which carried the implication, "you are to receive a gift; God is about to shower you with a special benefit."

Jesus was to be **called "the Son of God."** To be **called** meant not only to have a name attached but to *be* what the term signifies. The Jewish listeners understood this to mean that in Jesus all the character of God would come to expression.

Holy means to be set aside for God's service, often with the sense of purity; to be free of sin.

Jesus in Hebrew means "the Lord is salvation."

The Most High was a favorite title for God.

DISCUSSION GUIDELINES

Discussions go better when each person:

1. Respects the value of everyone's observations or insights
2. Allows everyone the opportunity to speak, if they so choose
3. Focuses the discussion on the passage being studied
4. Shares freely, but refrains from correcting or giving advice
5. Keeps all personal sharing confidential
6. Puts unanswered questions on the "Future Study List"

STEP ONE: **RESEARCH** FOR FACTS	*Luke 1:26-38* **A UNIQUE BEGINNING**	STEP TWO: **REVIEW** FOR MEANING
WHO is involved?	[26]In the sixth month the angel Gabriel was sent by God to a town in Galilee called Nazareth, [27]to a virgin engaged to a man whose name was Joseph, of the house of David. The virgin's name was Mary. [28]And he came to her and said, "Greetings, favored one! The Lord is with you." [29]But she was much perplexed by his words and pondered what sort of greeting this might be. [30]The angel said to her, "Do not be	**REPETITION:** Same words?
WHAT is happening?	afraid, Mary, for you have found favor with God. [31]And now, you will conceive in your womb and bear a son, and you will name him Jesus. [32]He will be great, and will be called the Son of the Most High, and the Lord God will give to him the throne of his ancestor David. [33]He will reign over the house of Jacob forever, and of his kingdom there will be no end."	**CONTRAST/ OPPOSITES** (Tip: "But," "yet")
WHAT is said?	[34]Mary said to the angel, "How can this be, since I am a virgin?" [35]The angel said to her, "The Holy Spirit will come upon you, and the power of the Most High will overshadow you; therefore the child to be born will be holy; he will be called Son of God. [36]And now, your relative Elizabeth in her old age has also conceived a son; and this is the sixth month for her who was said to be barren. [37]For nothing will be	**COMPARISONS/ SIMILARITIES** (Tip: "As," "so also," "like")
HOW do people relate/respond?	impossible with God." [38]Then Mary said, "Here am I, the servant of the Lord; let it be with me according to your word." Then the angel departed from her.	
		KEY WORDS: Why so Important? (Tip: Reveals main point)
WHEN?		
WHERE? did this happen?		**SIGNIFICANCE or IMPLICATIONS**

STEP THREE: **RESPOND** FOR LIFE

A New Thought to Ponder . . .
Something to Be Thankful for . . .
A Change Needed . . .
An Example to Follow . . .

WHO CALMS THE SEA?

Background Information

Jesus spent the day teaching large crowds of people gathered along the shore of the Sea of Galilee. To avoid the press of the crowd, Jesus spoke from a fishing boat anchored just offshore. When evening comes and the crowd disperses, Jesus and his disciples (his twelve closest followers) use the boat to cross over to the other side of the sea. Several of Jesus' disciples are fishermen and experienced sailors.

The Lake or Sea of Galilee is located in a basin surrounded by high hills and mountains in northern Israel. Sudden, violent storms on this lake are common. The violent winds and large swells created by such storms could possibly sink the wooden fishing boats used by the local fishermen. The disciples seem to have good reason to be terrified.

DISCUSSION GUIDELINES

Discussions go better when each person:

1. Respects the value of everyone's observations or insights
2. Allows everyone the opportunity to speak, if they so choose
3. Focuses the discussion on the passage being studied
4. Shares freely, but refrains from correcting or giving advice
5. Keeps all personal sharing confidential
6. Puts unanswered questions on the "Future Study List"

STEP ONE: **RESEARCH** FOR FACTS	*Mark 4:35-41* **WHO CALMS THE SEA?**	STEP TWO: **REVIEW** FOR MEANING
WHO is involved?	[35]On that day, when evening had come, he said to them, "Let us go across to the other side." [36]And leaving the crowd behind, they took him with them in the boat, just as he was. Other boats were with him. [37]A great windstorm arose, and the waves beat into the boat, so that the boat was already being swamped. [38]But he was in the stern, asleep on the cushion; and they woke him up and said to him, "Teacher, do you not care that we are perishing?" [39]He woke up and rebuked the wind, and said to the sea, "Peace! Be still!" Then the wind ceased, and there was a dead calm. [40]He said to them, "Why are you afraid? Have you still no faith?" [41]And they were filled with great awe and said to one another, "Who then is this, that even the wind and the sea obey him?"	**REPETITION:** Same words?
WHAT is happening?		**CONTRAST/ OPPOSITES** (Tip: "But," "yet")
WHAT is said?		**COMPARISONS/ SIMILARITIES** (Tip: "As," "so also," "like")
HOW do people relate/respond?		**KEY WORDS:** Why so Important? (Tip: Reveals main point)
WHEN?		
WHERE? did this happen?		**SIGNIFICANCE or IMPLICATIONS**

STEP THREE: **RESPOND** FOR LIFE

A New Thought to Ponder . . .
Something to Be Thankful for . . .
A Change Needed . . .
An Example to Follow . . .

65

Mark 2:1-12
WHO CAN FORGIVE?

Background Information

In chapter 1 of his Gospel, Mark shows us how Jesus' fame grew. In chapter 2, he begins to introduce us to Jesus' critics and how he handled opposition. This event introduces us to the conflict he encountered with many religious leaders of his day. He was likely speaking to a crowd which had gathered in and around a house where he was staying.

Homes of this period were often constructed with flat roofs composed of several layers. Wooden beams were laid across the top of the house walls, then covered with layers of brush, mud or clay tiles, and finally grass. To make an opening in such a roof was not difficult. The roof could be reached by stairs along the side of the house. This design created a sturdy surface where many activities took place, including laundry, drying fruit, prayer and religious celebrations.

For Clarification

Scribes were religious leaders who were experts in the interpretation of Jewish Law and its application to every aspect of life. They saw themselves as defending God's honor. Their interpretations became a second law rivaling the Old Testament law.

Son of Man was a title by which Jesus referred to himself. The term would have carried significance as a title for the "Messiah," the liberator and king for whom the Jews were eagerly awaiting.

Blasphemy is irreverent, profane, impious speech about God. Its penalty in Old Testament times was death (Leviticus 24:16).

First-century Hebrews considered the **heart** to be the center for intellectual activity.

DISCUSSION GUIDELINES

Discussions go better when each person:

1. Respects the value of everyone's observations or insights
2. Allows everyone the opportunity to speak, if they so choose
3. Focuses the discussion on the passage being studied
4. Shares freely, but refrains from correcting or giving advice
5. Keeps all personal sharing confidential
6. Puts unanswered questions on the "Future Study List"

STEP ONE: **RESEARCH** FOR FACTS	*Mark 2:1-12* **WHO CAN FORGIVE?**	STEP TWO: **REVIEW** FOR MEANING
WHO is involved?	[1]When he returned to Capernaum after some days, it was reported that he was at home. [2]So many gathered around that there was no longer room for them, not even in front of the door; and he was speaking the word to them. [3]Then some people came, bringing to him a paralyzed man, carried by four of them. [4]And when they could not bring him to Jesus because of the crowd, they removed the roof above him; and after having dug through it, they let down the mat on which the paralytic lay. [5]When Jesus saw their faith, he said to the paralytic, "Son, your sins are forgiven." [6]Now some of the scribes were sitting there, questioning in their hearts, [7]"Why does this fellow speak in this way? It is blasphemy! Who can forgive sins but God alone?" [8]At once Jesus perceived in his spirit that they were discussing these questions among themselves; and he said to them, "Why do you raise such questions in your hearts? [9]Which is easier, to say to the paralytic, 'Your sins are forgiven,' or to say, 'Stand up and take your mat and walk'? [10]But so that you may know that the Son of Man has authority on earth to forgive sins" —he said to the paralytic— [11]"I say to you, stand up, take your mat and go to your home." [12]And he stood up, and immediately took the mat and went out before all of them; so that they were all amazed and glorified God, saying, "We have never seen anything like this!"	**REPETITION:** Same words?
WHAT is happening?		**CONTRAST/ OPPOSITES** (Tip: "But," "yet")
WHAT is said?		**COMPARISONS/ SIMILARITIES** (Tip: "As," "so also," "like")
HOW do people relate/respond?		**KEY WORDS:** Why so Important? (Tip: Reveals main point)
WHEN?		
WHERE? did this happen?		**SIGNIFICANCE or IMPLICATIONS**

STEP THREE: **RESPOND** FOR LIFE

A New Thought to Ponder . . .
Something to Be Thankful for . . .
A Change Needed . . .
An Example to Follow . . .

67

Mark 9:14-27
WHO COMMANDS THE SPIRITS?

Background Information

A man has brought his demon-possessed son to nine of Jesus' disciples, seeking healing for the boy. The father fully expects these disciples can heal his son since the Jews believe "the messenger of a man is as the man himself." In Jesus' absence, the disciples stand in his place and are regarded as he is, so they should have the same power as Jesus.

A crowd has gathered around the disciples. Religious leaders are among the crowd, watching to see what will happen, possibly checking to be sure that no religious laws are broken. Into this scene, Jesus and three other disciples arrive. Jesus' expression of exasperation reflects a weariness close to heartbreak and is addressed personally to the disciples.

For Clarification

Teacher is equivalent to "Rabbi."

Scribes were religious leaders who were specialists in the interpretation of the Jewish law.

DISCUSSION GUIDELINES

Discussions go better when each person:

1. Respects the value of everyone's observations or insights
2. Allows everyone the opportunity to speak, if they so choose
3. Focuses the discussion on the passage being studied
4. Shares freely, but refrains from correcting or giving advice
5. Keeps all personal sharing confidential
6. Puts unanswered questions on the "Future Study List"

STEP ONE: **RESEARCH** FOR FACTS	*Mark 9:14-27* **WHO COMMANDS THE SPIRITS?**	STEP TWO: **REVIEW** FOR MEANING
WHO is involved?	[14]When they came to the disciples, they saw a great crowd around them, and some scribes arguing with them. [15]When the whole crowd saw him, they were immediately overcome with awe, and they ran forward to greet him. [16]He asked them, "What are you arguing about with them?" [17]Someone from the crowd answered him, "Teacher, I brought you my son; he has a spirit that makes him unable to speak; [18]and whenever it seizes him, it dashes him down; and he foams and grinds his teeth and becomes rigid; and I asked your disciples to cast it out, but they could not do so." [19]He answered them, "You faithless generation, how much longer must I be among you? How much longer must I put up with you? Bring him to me." [20]And they brought the boy to him. When the spirit saw him, immediately it convulsed the boy, and he fell on the ground and rolled about, foaming at the mouth. [21]Jesus asked the father, "How long has this been happening to him?" And he said, "From childhood. [22]It has often cast him into the fire and into the water, to destroy him; but if you are able to do anything, have pity on us and help us." [23]Jesus said to him, "If you are able!—All things can be done for the one who believes." [24]Immediately the father of the child cried out, "I believe; help my unbelief!" [25]When Jesus saw that a crowd came running together, he rebuked the unclean spirit, saying to it, "You spirit that keeps this boy from speaking and hearing, I command you, come out of him, and never enter him again!" [26]After crying out and convulsing him terribly, it came out, and the boy was like a corpse, so that most of them said, "He is dead." [27]But Jesus took him by the hand and lifted him up, and he was able to stand.	**REPETITION:** Same words?
WHAT is happening?		**CONTRAST/ OPPOSITES** (Tip: "But," "yet")
WHAT is said?		**COMPARISONS/ SIMILARITIES** (Tip: "As," "so also," "like")
HOW do people relate/respond?		**KEY WORDS:** Why so Important? (Tip: Reveals main point)
WHEN?		
WHERE? did this happen?		**SIGNIFICANCE or IMPLICATIONS**

STEP THREE: **RESPOND** FOR LIFE

A New Thought to Ponder . . .
Something to Be Thankful for . . .
A Change Needed . . .
An Example to Follow . . .

69

Luke 7:11-17
WHO RAISES THE DEAD?

Background Information

During the first century the dead were buried outside the city. Jesus met this funeral procession at the city gate, just as he was entering and they were leaving the city.

This was likely a desperate situation for the woman, a widow about to bury her only son. He was her sole mainstay in a society where a woman alone had no way to support herself. Women were provided for only through the work of their fathers, husbands, or sons. Now this woman was likely destitute.

It was very unusual for Jesus, a well-know rabbi, to stop this funeral procession and shocking that he would touch the coffin or stretcher since contact with the dead defiled any Jewish person. It was also unusual that a rabbi would stop and speak to a woman.

For Clarification

A **coffin** in the first century was more like a stretcher on which the dead man, probably only covered by a cloth, was carried to a tomb.

Judea was a region in the south of Israel.

Nain was a village a few miles southeast of Nazareth in the hills, surrounded by caves used for burials.

DISCUSSION GUIDELINES

Discussions go better when each person:

    1. Respects the value of everyone's observations or insights
    2. Allows everyone the opportunity to speak, if they so choose
    3. Focuses the discussion on the passage being studied
    4. Shares freely, but refrains from correcting or giving advice
    5. Keeps all personal sharing confidential
    6. Puts unanswered questions on the "Future Study List"

STEP ONE: **RESEARCH** FOR FACTS	*Luke 7:11-17* **WHO RAISES THE DEAD?**	STEP TWO: **REVIEW** FOR MEANING
WHO is involved?	[11]Soon afterward, Jesus went to a town called Nain, and his disciples and a large crowd went along with him. [12]As he approached the town gate, a dead person was being carried out—the only son of his mother, and she was a widow. And a large crowd from the town was with her. [13]When the Lord saw her, his heart went out to her and he said, "Don't cry."	**REPETITION:** Same words?
WHAT is happening?	[14]Then he went up and touched the coffin, and those carrying it stood still. He said "Young man, I say to you, get up!" [15]The dead man sat up and began to talk, and Jesus gave him back to his mother.	**CONTRAST/ OPPOSITES** (Tip: "But," "yet")
WHAT is said?	[16]They were filled with awe and praised God. "A great prophet has appeared among us," they said. "God has come to help his people." [17]This news about Jesus spread throughout Judea and the surrounding country. (NIV)	**COMPARISONS/ SIMILARITIES** (Tip: "As," "so also," "like")
HOW do people relate/respond?		**KEY WORDS:** Why so Important? (Tip: Reveals main point)
WHEN?		
WHERE? did this happen?		**SIGNIFICANCE or IMPLICATIONS**

STEP THREE: **RESPOND** FOR LIFE

A New Thought to Ponder . . .
Something to Be Thankful for . . .
A Change Needed . . .
An Example to Follow . . .

John 11:20-44
WHO WILL NEVER DIE?

Background Information
This event involves very close friends of Jesus: Mary, Martha, and Lazarus. They had on many occasions opened their home to Jesus, providing not only friendship but meals and housing. By the time Jesus arrived at their home this time, Lazarus had been dead for four days.

First-century Jews believed that when anyone died, the soul of the dead person lingered near the body for three days. But by the fourth day the soul had left. This meant that there was no longer any possibility that the soul would reenter the body and recovery of the person take place. Four days of death meant the person would stay dead. Every last hope for Lazarus was gone by the time Jesus arrived.

Traveling from Jerusalem to Bethany, where Lazarus was buried, was dangerous for Jesus and his disciples. It brought them into a region where the Jewish leaders had recently attempted to kill Jesus. He had offended the Jewish religious leaders on many occasions, and by this point many of them were trying to have him arrested or killed.

For Clarification

The **Pharisees** were Jewish religious leaders, many of whom opposed Jesus.

The **Messiah** was the expected king and deliverer of the Jews. The Hebrew word "Messiah" is interchangeable with the Greek word "Christ." Martha had come to believe that Jesus was the long-awaited Messiah come from God to save his people.

Lord is a title of diety, acknowledging that Jesus was indeed the living God.

To **believe** is to be persuaded of, to rely upon, to place confidence in; it is not mere acknowledgement.

Life is life which lasts through all eternity and comes from Christ.

Jesus is the author of the power of **resurrection**, which is a raising from the dead to eternal life.

DISCUSSION GUIDELINES
Discussions go better when each person:

1. Respects the value of everyone's observations or insights
2. Allows everyone the opportunity to speak, if they so choose
3. Focuses the discussion on the passage being studied
4. Shares freely, but refrains from correcting or giving advice
5. Keeps all personal sharing confidential
6. Puts unanswered questions on the "Future Study List"

STEP ONE: **RESEARCH** FOR FACTS	*John 11:20-44* **WHO WILL NEVER DIE?**	STEP TWO: **REVIEW** FOR MEANING
WHO is involved?	[20]When Martha heard that Jesus was coming, she went and met him, while Mary stayed at home. [21]Martha said to Jesus, "Lord, if you had been here, my brother would not have died. [22]But even now I know that God will give you whatever you ask of him." [23]Jesus said to her, "Your brother will rise again." [24]Martha said to him, "I know that he will rise again in the resurrection on the last day." [25]Jesus said to her, "I am the resurrection and the life.	**REPETITION:** Same words?
WHAT is happening?	Those who believe in me, even though they die, will live, [26]and everyone who lives and believes in me will never die. Do you believe this?" [27]She said to him, "Yes, Lord, I believe that you are the Messiah, the Son of God, the one coming into the world."	**CONTRAST/ OPPOSITES** (Tip: "But," "yet")
WHAT is said?	[28]When she had said this, she went back and called her sister Mary, and told her privately, "The Teacher is here and is calling for you." [29]And when she heard it, she got up quickly and went to him. [30]Now Jesus had not yet come to the village, but was still at the place where Martha had met him. [31]The Jews who were with her in the house, consoling her, saw Mary get up quickly and go out. They followed her because they thought that she was going to the tomb to weep there. [32]When Mary came where Jesus was and saw him, she knelt at his feet and said to him, "Lord, if you had been here, my brother would not have died." [33]When Jesus saw her	**COMPARISONS/ SIMILARITIES** (Tip: "As," "so also," "like")
HOW do people relate/respond?	weeping, and the Jews who came with her also weeping, he was greatly disturbed in spirit and deeply moved. [34]He said, "Where have you laid him?" They said to him, "Lord, come and see." [35]Jesus began to weep. [36]So the Jews said, "See how he loved him!" [37]But some of them said, "Could not he who opened the eyes of the blind man have kept this man from dying?"	**KEY WORDS:** Why so Important? (Tip: Reveals main point)
WHEN?	[38]Then Jesus, again greatly disturbed, came to the tomb. It was a cave, and a stone was lying against it. [39]Jesus said, "Take away the stone." Martha, the sister of the dead man, said to him, "Lord, already there is a stench because he has been dead four days." [40]Jesus said to her, "Did I not tell you that if you believed, you would see the glory of God?" [41]So they took away the stone. And Jesus looked upward and said, "Father, I thank you for having heard me. [42]I knew that you always hear me, but I have said	
WHERE? did this happen?	this for the sake of the crowd standing here, so that they may believe that you sent me." [43]When he had said this, he cried with a loud voice, "Lazarus, come out!" [44]The dead man came out, his hands and feet bound with strips of cloth, and his face wrapped in a cloth. Jesus said to them, "Unbind him, and let him go."	**SIGNIFICANCE or IMPLICATIONS**

STEP THREE: **RESPOND** FOR LIFE

A New Thought to Ponder . . .
Something to Be Thankful for . . .
A Change Needed . . .
An Example to Follow . . .

73

Matthew 28:1-15
WHERE IS HE?

Background Information

These women, considered disciples or followers of Jesus, come to visit the tomb where Jesus is buried. They may be following a first-century Jewish tradition of visiting the tombs of the deceased until the third day to ensure the person is truly dead.

Claiming the resurrection of Jesus to be a hoax is not a recent idea. During the time of Jesus' earthly life, many people refused to believe who he was. The Jewish leaders who refused to believe in his resurrection could only conclude that the body had been stolen right under the eyes of the armed Roman guards. But molesting graves was a serious offense in first-century culture, punishable at times by death. It is not likely that the frightened disciples who were hiding behind locked doors would risk death to tamper with the tomb.

For Clarification

Worshiped can mean "knelt before" as an act of reverence.

Mary Magdalene was one of the most prominent women of Galilee to follow Jesus.

A **stone** was used in the first century to seal a tomb.

Galilee is a region in northern Palestine primarily inhabited by non-Jewish peoples. Jesus spent considerable time there.

DISCUSSION GUIDELINES

Discussions go better when each person:

1. Respects the value of everyone's observations or insights
2. Allows everyone the opportunity to speak, if they so choose
3. Focuses the discussion on the passage being studied
4. Shares freely, but refrains from correcting or giving advice
5. Keeps all personal sharing confidential
6. Puts unanswered questions on the "Future Study List"

STEP ONE: **RESEARCH** FOR FACTS	*Matthew 28:1-15* **WHERE IS HE?**	STEP TWO: **REVIEW** FOR MEANING
WHO is involved?	[1]After the sabbath, at dawn on the first day of the week, Mary Magdalene and the other Mary went to look at the tomb. [2]There was a violent earthquake, for an angel of the Lord came down from heaven and, going to the tomb, rolled back the stone and sat on it. [3]His appearance was like lightning, and his clothes were white as snow. [4]The guards were so afraid of him that they shook and became like dead men.	**REPETITION:** Same words?
WHAT is happening?	[5]The angel said to the women, "Do not be afraid, for I know that you are looking for Jesus, who was crucified. [6]He is not here; he has risen, just as he said. Come and see the place where he lay. [7]Then go quickly and tell his disciples: 'He has risen from the dead and is going ahead of you into Galilee. There you will see him.' Now I have told you."	**CONTRAST/ OPPOSITES** (Tip: "But," "yet")
WHAT is said?	[8]So the women hurried away from the tomb, afraid yet filled with joy, and ran to tell his disciples. [9]Suddenly Jesus met them. "Greetings," he said. They came to him, clasped his feet and worshiped him. [10]Then Jesus said to them, "Do not be afraid. Go and tell my brothers to go to Galilee; there they will see me."	**COMPARISONS/ SIMILARITIES** (Tip: "As," "so also," "like")
HOW do people relate/respond?	[11]While the women were on their way, some of the guards went into the city and reported to the chief priests everything that had happened. [12]When the chief priests had met with the elders and devised a plan, they gave the soldiers a large sum of money, [13]telling them, "You are to say, 'His disciples came during the night and stole him away while we were asleep.' [14]If this report gets to the governor, we will satisfy him and keep you out of trouble." [15]So the soldiers took the money and did as they were instructed. And this story has been widely circulated among the Jews to this very day. (NIV)	**KEY WORDS:** Why so Important? (Tip: Reveals main point)
WHEN?		
WHERE? did this happen?		**SIGNIFICANCE or IMPLICATIONS**

STEP THREE: **RESPOND** FOR LIFE

A New Thought to Ponder . . .
Something to Be Thankful for . . .
A Change Needed . . .
An Example to Follow . . .

John 20:24-31
I WILL NOT BELIEVE . . . UNLESS

Background Information

On the day Jesus rose from the dead, he made several different appearances. Many of his disciples witnessed one of these appearances, but not Thomas.

Although Thomas had lived with this group of disciples for years and knew them as trustworthy people, he was not willing to believe them when they claimed to have seen Jesus. Like many throughout history, Thomas was convinced that dead men don't rise. Since Thomas would not be easily convinced, certainly not by the report of others, he demanded to see firsthand the marks of the crucifixion on the body of Jesus.

For Clarification

The Twelve were the original disciples who followed Jesus throughout his earthly ministry.

If **the doors were shut**, it was understood that they were locked.

The Messiah was the expected king and deliverer of the Jews. The Hebrew word "Messiah" is interchangeable with the Greek word "Christ."

Lord is a title of diety, acknowledging that Jesus was indeed the living God.

To **believe** is to be persuaded of, to rely upon, to place confidence in. It is not mere acknowledgment.

Life is life which lasts through all eternity and which comes from Christ.

DISCUSSION GUIDELINES

Discussions go better when each person:

1. Respects the value of everyone's observations or insights
2. Allows everyone the opportunity to speak, if they so choose
3. Focuses the discussion on the passage being studied
4. Shares freely, but refrains from correcting or giving advice
5. Keeps all personal sharing confidential
6. Puts unanswered questions on the "Future Study List"

STEP ONE: **RESEARCH** FOR FACTS	*John 20:24-31* **I WILL NOT BELIEVE . . . UNLESS**	STEP TWO: **REVIEW** FOR MEANING
WHO is involved?	[24]But Thomas (who was called the Twin), one of the twelve, was not with them when Jesus came. [25]So the other disciples told him, "We have seen the Lord." But he said to them, "Unless I see the mark of the nails in his hands, and put my finger in the mark of the nails and my hand in his side, I will not believe."	**REPETITION:** Same words?
WHAT is happening?	[26]A week later his disciples were again in the house, and Thomas was with them. Although the doors were shut, Jesus came and stood among them and said, "Peace be with you!" [27]Then he said to Thomas, "Put your finger here and see my hands. Reach out your hand and put it in my side. Do not doubt but believe." [28]Thomas answered him, "My Lord and my God!" [29]Jesus said to him, "Have you believed because you have seen me? Blessed are those who have not seen and yet have come to believe."	**CONTRAST/ OPPOSITES** (Tip: "But," "yet")
WHAT is said?	[30]Now Jesus did many other signs in the presence of his disciples, which are not written in this book. [31]But these are written so that you may come to believe that Jesus is the Messiah, the Son of God, and that through believing you may have life in his name.	**COMPARISONS/ SIMILARITIES** (Tip: "As," "so also," "like")
HOW do people relate/respond?		**KEY WORDS:** Why so Important? (Tip: Reveals main point)
WHEN?		
WHERE? did this happen?		**SIGNIFICANCE or IMPLICATIONS**

STEP THREE: **RESPOND** FOR LIFE

A New Thought to Ponder . . .
Something to Be Thankful for . . .
A Change Needed . . .
An Example to Follow . . .

chapter six
TROUBLESHOOTER'S GUIDE FOR EFFECTIVE DISCUSSIONS

The word *discussion* means that at least two people are engaged in a lively exchange of ideas. A conversational Bible study discussion leader plays a key role in facilitating a focused dialogue.

FACILITATING FOCUSED DISCUSSIONS

1. Trust the Holy Spirit to teach you and others. Remember Jesus' words to his disciples: "The Holy Spirit, whom the Father will send in my name, will teach you all things . . ." (John 14:26).

2. Bring a spirit of anticipation to the study. Your eagerness to learn will be contagious!

3. Guard against quickly answering your own discussion questions. People need time to organize their thoughts before they can respond.

4. Acknowledge people's contributions, and stimulate dialogue by inviting them to explain their observations more fully.

5. Participate in the discussion, but be careful to follow the discussion groundrules: don't dominate, teach, advise, or correct. Share *briefly* your observations, insights or meaning for your own life. Your sharing can be a model to encourage others to express their view.

6. Stay with the clear facts of the passage. Avoid tangents or lengthy discussions about unclear points. Write difficult, tangential, or unanswerable questions on your Future Study List.

7. Allow discussion to move spontaneously, rather than asking each person to speak or "going around the circle." Encourage people to converse with each other rather than answering you directly.

FOSTERING CONVERSATION BY RESPONDING WITH OPEN-ENDED QUESTIONS

At times people give very brief responses to good questions. You can encourage lively conversation about the passage and affirm any comment by using open-ended follow-up questions, such as:

- "Greg, I've never seen it that way before; could you elaborate your point a bit?"

- "What additional details can be discovered from this passage about what Steve just said?"

- "Are there other ideas about the significance of . . . ?"

- "Susan, tell us more about what you're thinking."

- "These are good observations—does anyone have another perspective to add?"

Avoid asking questions that have only yes or no answers. Strive for an accepting, inquisitive, respectful tone and attitude in your responses.

MANAGING A VERBALLY DOMINANT PERSON PRODUCTIVELY

There are many reasons why a person may dominate the discussion. Some people learn best by "thinking out loud." Others may be naturally exuberant. Some feel they are helping by "filling in" the silences. Still others may seek affirmation or attention. Whatever the person's reason for dominating, to foster good discussion you may need to take steps to prevent that person from controlling the conversation. Others may become frustrated and lose interest in the discussion if it becomes a monologue.

First, try non-verbal cues to divert attention away from the dominant or verbal person. Continual eye contact can encourage continual talking. Instead, look at other group members or down at your papers. Sit next to the dominant person, if possible, with the quieter people in your direct line of vision.

Actively solicit input from others as soon as a verbal person finishes a sentence. You might say something like "I'd like to hear what some of the rest of you think. Deborah, you appear to have a thought on the tip of your tongue."

When you are dealing with people who like to think out loud or have trouble speaking concisely, don't be afraid to interrupt them and help them finish their thought.

If these approaches don't moderate the verbally dominating, take the person aside privately and explain that you would like his or her help to draw out comments from the other people since the goal of the study is discussion. Explain that you purposely allow silences to help people think. This approach can help the person realize how others are different and understand your comfort with silence. It can also give the more naturally verbal members a sense of partnership with you and the common goal of fostering discussion. As you prepare, focus your prayers for the verbal and quieter people that the Spirit will encourage each to contribute with respect for others.

TREATING THE QUIETER PERSON WITH CARE

Just as there are many reasons for verbally dominant behavior, so there are many reasons people remain quiet in a group. Some people learn best by quietly thinking for a while before they are ready to speak. Others may hold back because they are timid, because they are afraid to give a wrong answer, or because they think their observations are not significant or have already been said. Allow time for quiet people to feel comfortable in the group.

Carefully observe a quiet person's facial expressions and body language. You can learn to tell the difference between someone who is eager to speak but needs an invitation to do so, and someone who prefers to listen and absorb and is not ready to speak.

Affirm quiet people by using eye contact and by expressing your confidence in their contributions to the group. Avoid drawing undue attention to their quietness. Never assume quieter people have nothing to share, or that they have no desire to speak. Often, they just need a thoughtful prompt or invitation to share their thoughts. You could say, "Pat, it appears you've been thinking very hard—do you have something you'd like to share?" If the response is "no," say, "That's fine. I was just curious." If "yes," be very sure to affirm what is shared by an appropriate follow-up question, such as, "Thanks for expressing your thoughts; does anyone else have a similar or different observation?" Remember, the goal is not to get everyone to talk; the goal is to encourage the value of each person's perspective.

HANDLING COMMENTS THAT SEEM UNRELATED OR "WRONG"

First, don't be too quick to judge the person's response. Think about the comment, and allow others to think too. It may have more merit than you initially thought.

Many seemingly "wrong" answers may be modified by other observations as the study progresses. Don't fall into the role of a corrective teacher. Learn to trust the Spirit for timing, teaching, or correcting.

Thank the person for expressing his or her views. Then choose an option for guiding everyone back into the facts of the passage *without* correcting the person. You have several options, depending on how insistent the person is that his or her insight is right or the best:

- You could ask the person to explain his or her point of view more fully, and how the conclusions were drawn from the passage. A possible response could be: "That's an interesting perspective, Sandy. Can you tell us more about how you came to that conclusion from this passage?"

- You can invite other people to respond with observations from the passage. You can say, "Does anyone have a similar or different perspective?"

- You can give your opinion just as others would give theirs, not as a teacher correcting or pronouncing judgment. You do not want to close down the discussion and diminish participation. Use "I" statements, such as, "Your point is intriguing. I have never seen it that way. For me, this passage seems to say. . . ."

- You can close that part of the discussion by stating, "That's an interesting point of view. Because our time is limited, let's go to the next question in this Step."

- You can agree to meet later to discuss the person's point of view or suggest the point be put on the "Future Study List" for research later. For example, "John, your point is very important. Since there seems to be no answer in this passage, could you and I discuss it together later, or shall we put it on our "Future Study List"?

RESPONDING TO SOMEONE WHO INSISTS ON USING A DIFFERENT TRANSLATION

These studies use a printed manuscript format for a specific purpose. The goal is to foster a community of people looking at the same words, with the same helps, with the option to analyze by marking on the same study sheet.

Some people have strong feelings about certain translations and about using their own Bibles. While you do not want to prevent anyone from participating because of the format, first ask the person to try the Bible study sheet once to see how it goes and for the sake of everyone else. Most people will agree and usually discover they were able to learn things they never saw before using the manuscript format. If they insist on using their version or their Bible, invite them to refrain from referring to any notes in the Bible which others do not have and from discussing particular word variances. These can sidetrack the discussion.

HANDLING THE "EXPERT" OR ADVICE GIVER

Some people tend to declare the definitive meaning of a passage. They may feel a need for clear-cut answers and closure. Some people feel uncomfortable in a group with a discussion facilitator rather than with a teacher in control. They may want to step in and be the expert or give advice.

The difficulty with this behavior is that it may not communicate respect for others' insights and it inhibits learning in community. If someone takes the expert or advisor role, you can respond, "Thanks Jeffrey, that is one possible way of looking at this passage. How do others of you view this passage?" or "Perhaps it's a good time to remember our Discussion Guidelines about not giving advice and respecting others' views."

RESPONDING WHEN PEOPLE REFER TO AN OUTSIDE AUTHORITY FOR "THE ANSWER"

Someone may refer to an outside authority (such as a pastor or book) that has taught the "correct" meaning of the passage being studied. This person may assume that "the answer" has been given by the authority, so discussion is pointless. This situation is very similar to the problem of the expert described above, and can be handled in a similar fashion. A helpful response might be, "Thank you, Jennifer, for sharing that with us. There certainly is value to what we can learn from the teaching of others. However, our purpose in these Bible discussions is to dig into the passage for ourselves and see what new discoveries we can make with the help of the Holy Spirit, and to try not to rely on the study of others."

AVOIDING THE TEMPTATION TO TEACH INSTEAD OF FACILITATE

Some people are used to the leader having the "right" answers or the correct teaching. The conversational Bible study method relies heavily on the Holy Spirit revealing insights to and through any member of the group and deepening discoveries by meaty discussion. Whenever anyone assumes a teacher role, the discovery and discussion are inhibited or sometimes halted. Some tips for remaining a facilitator and avoiding teaching are:

- Recognize how easy and enticing it is to tell the answers instead of encouraging the discoveries of others.

- Remind yourself and others of the Holy Spirit's work to teach each one of us.

- Be comfortable with unanswered questions. People often really learn when they discover for themselves at the right moment.

- Encourage all in the group to share the responsibility for discovering answers.

- Be sensitive to when the Spirit is nudging you to contribute insights or answers, and do so with words like "I see it this way," "For me, this seems to make sense," or, "My view is similar to what Steve said . . ." rather than with definitive pronouncements. Follow up with, "What do you think?"

- Remember to place questions not answered in the passage on the "Future Study List" and ask for volunteers to research for answers. You can suggest that church libraries have Bible dictionaries, commentaries, or Bible handbooks.

RESISTING PREMATURE DISCUSSION OF APPLICATION

Some people may tend to move past Steps One and Two of the study and jump immediately to personal response (Step Three). At times, quick conclusions may not be true to the real meaning of Scripture.

Encourage the group to dig carefully for all the important facts before drawing conclusions. It may take time for people to learn how to put "study" before "application." You can graciously express appreciation for the application shared and affirm the observation by saying, "You are quick! That's what we need to think about in Step Three. For now, let's finish Step One (or Step Two)."

HELPING PARTICIPANTS MOVE FROM STUDY TO RESPONSE

Some people have difficulty making the leap from mental study to personal application for everyday life. You can help by choosing an Option in Step Three that is more obvious or relates well to what people have shared.

If the concept of responding for life is new to your group, or if you are facilitating a study with people who would not consider themselves believers, you may want to begin by asking them to write or think about their responses instead of encouraging them to share openly.

Sharing your own personal response from Step Three in a way that models appropriate openness can help people develop their own responses.

Good follow-up questions can also help. When a person gives a general response to a Respond for Life question (Step Three), you may want to ask, "Would you want to share how that insight affects your everyday life?" Don't push if the response is "no" or "I'm not sure."

Again, remember the Holy Spirit can be counted on to reveal insights and personal responses for each person. He knows people's hearts and how they learn and respond best. Enjoy watching the Spirit work in quiet and exciting ways.

Chapter seven

USING RADICAL RELATIONSHIPS STUDIES IN SPECIAL SETTINGS

IN THE MARKETPLACE

RADICAL RELATIONSHIPS Bible studies are ideal for use among coworkers or in workplace settings. *Jesus' Farewell Teachings* is most effective with those who have a serious interest in studying the Bible—new or long-time followers of Christ. *The Uniqueness of Jesus* and *Jesus on Relationships* in this series are preferable for those who are just beginning to seek to know God or are curious about the Bible. In addition:

- These studies are easy for busy people to use with only brief preparation by the leader.

- Each study stands on its own so people can attend as they are able without losing the flow of the studies.

- The studies focus on the person and teachings of Jesus and do not attempt to teach any particular doctrine.

- No prior Bible knowledge is needed to participate meaningfully in the studies. Everyone has the same background information and the same Bible passage.

- The studies are flexible both in amount of time for a study (60- or 30-minute format) and in discussion options, tailored to needs of marketplace people.

When using RADICAL RELATIONSHIPS in a marketplace setting:

1. Be sensitive to include those who may not be long-time followers of Jesus. Use language that will be understood by everyone instead of Christian terms. Guard against talking only with one or two friends whom you know are Christians. Ask for the Spirit's sensitivity to those who are spiritually searching. These studies offer seekers a great opportunity to discover the person of Jesus.

2. Be sensitive to office relationships as you invite people. Think about the relationship dynamics and management style of your workplace. If people tend to interact freely in the work setting, you may invite managers and non-managers to participate in the same group. If not, consider limiting your invitation to people with similar responsibility.

3. Choose a convenient time and non-threatening location. (See the story of Patricia's marketplace group on pages 15-16.) Be sure to consider company policies concerning non-work-related meetings in the office or during the workday. If your company has written policies against such meetings, or they are contrary to the culture, hold your meetings off-site or after hours.

If you meet in a company meeting room, check to see if there are restrictions on the times and places you can meet. If you meet in a restaurant or other public meeting place, consider choosing a time or location where you will not be distracted by crowds or high noise levels.

4. Invite coworkers tactfully. You may decide that personal invitations are the best way to let people know of the opportunity. Depending on the size and personality of your company, employee bulletin boards or newsletters may also be an appropriate way to find interested people.

5. Keep discussion of Step Three (Respond for Life) general and non-threatening. Let the people set the tone and level of intimacy. If the people in your group are friends as well as coworkers, your discussions may naturally become more personal. Be careful to avoid negative discussion of company policies or employee behavior.

If you have both management and non-management employees involved in your study, be aware of the work-related environment where managers may feel uncomfortable discussing certain issues with non-managers, and vice versa. This may be especially important if the discussion turns to issues of power and authority.

6. Be sensitive to time constraints. The people you involve in your study will almost certainly be very busy, with many demands on their time. Start and end each session on time. Get down to business quickly. Keep the studies moving at a steady pace.

7. Be persistent, but flexible. You might have better attendance if you give each person regular reminders of meeting times and places. However, understand and accept the pressures and deadlines that may keep people from attending every meeting or cause them to drop out altogether. Be prepared for people to arrive late or leave early. Encourage people that missing a study doesn't prevent their future involvement. Explain that each RADICAL RELATIONSHIPS study can stand on its own, and people will not feel out of place if they miss several studies.

8. If you are leading a group in an office where you do not work, enlist someone who works in that office as a co-sponsor. This person can give you valuable insights into the atmosphere and policies of the company, and can be your in-house contact to invite people. Most companies will not allow events such as a Bible study to be held in their facilities unless the program is sponsored by an employee.

IN MULTICULTURAL GROUPS

RADICAL RELATIONSHIPS Bible studies are ideal for groups of culturally diverse people. These studies:

- Require no previous Bible knowledge or understanding of Christianity
- Focus on personal discoveries and discussion, so diverse people can contribute out of their unique perspectives
- Allow people unfamiliar with the Bible to investigate portions of Scripture first-hand
- Can contribute to building understanding among diverse people as they learn to listen and appreciate the unique perspective each brings to the study

Today we see all around us evidence of the increasing movement of diverse peoples to the U.S. The worldwide movement of people groups, the increase in immigration, and the return of foreign-born Americans to the U.S. are substantially changing the nation's cultural makeup. As we encounter people from different cultural and ethnic backgrounds, our "taken-for-granted" assumptions about what is good or bad, fair or unfair, and more important or less important will very likely be challenged.

As our neighborhoods and workplaces become increasingly diverse, we will likely encounter a sense of "culture-clash"—people from diverse cultural and ethnic backgrounds will clash in living out different approaches to work and relationships. Understanding a bit about culture and its pervasive influence on the way we think and behave may enable us to relate more caringly across the possible gulf of culture or ethnicity. This understanding can also help you more thoughtfully include diverse people in your RADICAL RELATIONSHIPS Bible studies.

Culture is a comprehensive system of ideas, feelings, and values that is shared by a group of people, and that influences their behavior and interpretation of people and events. Our culture affects every aspect of our lives. It shapes our basic beliefs about the world, our perceptions, values, tastes, behaviors, attitudes, and judgments. It affects the way we express ourselves, form relationships, approach our work, and judge right from wrong.

All people carry with them the permeating stamp of their own culture. As we become conscious of how our culture has shaped us, we can learn to modify some of its impact. But the deeply ingrained values we inherit from our culture are very difficult to change. Every culture believes that its values and ways of behaving are the *right* ones.

For example, Euro-Americans tend to see change as primarily good, linked to progress and growth. More traditional cultures value stability and heritage; they see change as disruptive. Euro-Americans tend to highly value productivity and think that schedules should be planned and followed. Other cultures, such as the Latino cultures, tend to value deep relationships more than efficiency or productivity. These two deeply held values can easily clash and cause conflict, rejection, and great personal pain.

When leading a study which includes people who are ethnically or culturally diverse:

1. Be sensitive to the natural human inclination to be with people most like yourself. We tend to converse more with people we know and/or have something in common with. The result may be to unconsciously exclude someone who is different.

2. Take steps to include the culturally diverse person by getting acquainted with him or her and introducing that person to others in the study.

3. Show that you value diverse perspectives. Your international or ethnic American friends will tend to bring different perspectives to the passage being studied. Because of their different points of view, they may feel hesitant to express their ideas. You may need to express to the group how much you value the different perspectives each person brings to the study of the Bible. This cultural diversity helps us gain a broader understanding of God's character. It is an exciting way to grow! Also allow each person the opportunity to listen only and not contribute verbally if they so desire.

4. Continue to grow in understanding the effects of your own culture on your values, attitudes, and behavior. Knowing your cultural biases will enable you to be more sensitive to cultural differences, and less inclined to judge people of different cultures or ethnic groups.

5. Seek to live out biblical hospitality, which expresses a spirit of welcoming and respecting those who are different from you.

6. Grow in your ability to treat people who are different as equals. Don't assume equal treatment is automatic. Our hidden biases tend to cause us to favor some people over others.

7. If you are speaking with a person who does not speak English fluently, speak more slowly and distinctly than you would with someone from your own culture. Be aware of the tendency to compensate for your friend's limited English by speaking loudly. This will likely embarrass you both. A person with limited English often must mentally move between two languages, and this translation takes time. Patiently allow time for this person to respond to your questions.

8. Different accents or limited English may make it difficult for you to understand a person's response fully. It's best not to pretend to understand. Rather, with sincere apology say, "I'm very sorry, but I did not fully understand your response. Would you be so kind as to repeat your response again?"

9. Remember that words are culturally shaped and do not typically carry the same meaning for everyone. Therefore, try to avoid words that could be seen as "insiders' lingo," especially common Christian phrases, such as "When were you saved? How are you growing? Who discipled you?" When necessary, explain the "insiders' lingo" to the "outsider."

10. Be sensitive to when it is acceptable to be direct and indirect. In some countries you are expected to speak in a straightforward manner, telling things as they appear to you. In other countries people are concerned with saving face; you would rarely tell people something directly, especially if you know more about a particular area than they do.

11. Learn to observe people. When two or more people from the same culture or ethnic group are together, notice their use of distance as they speak to each other. Pay attention to other nonverbal clues, such as eye contact, touching, and facial expressions. Your observations will help you communicate more effectively with these people.

12. Take time to build your friendship apart from the study. With your ethnic American or international friends, developing your relationship with them will tend to be important. It will help them feel more comfortable in the study. They will probably share more in the study if you invest in building the relationship apart from the study.

WITH SEEKERS
Experience has shown that people who are not yet believers in Jesus but who are interested in their own spirituality find the RADICAL RELATIONSHIPS format and style very refreshing. Because the style is conversational, people who are unfamiliar with the Bible seem to feel comfortable investigating a passage for themselves and expressing their views.

INVITING YOUR FRIENDS

1. Begin with people you already have a relationship with, either at work or in the community.

2. Let them know you are very interested in what they believe and how they think about spiritual things. Explain your interest in learning from the Bible, and invite them to experience a Bible discussion with you.

3. Emphasize the conversational nature of the study. Tell people it is a discussion about stories in the life of Jesus from the Bible. The concept of studying the Bible is generally foreign to a person not yet wanting to become a disciple of Jesus, but discussing their opinions is attractive.

4. Emphasize the discovery process and that you will not be teaching them what to believe or what the Bible says. They will be making their own discoveries.

5. Emphasize that they don't have to prepare, don't need to own a Bible and don't have to know anything about the Bible. The Bible passage, background information, and discussion questions are all printed right on the study sheet. You may find it best to photocopy the Bible Study and Background Information sheets the first time or two. (See page 11.)

6. Consider using the 30-minute format with seekers who may not be ready to give much time to Bible discussion, at least the first time.

7. Avoid asking them to commit to a number of weeks or sessions. Invite them just to try something new first and see if it interests them.

8. Challenge them to investigate the person of Jesus from the Bible to see if their view is different or the same.

Responses for the Resistant

1. "I don't really believe the Bible is true." Explain it is not necessary to believe the Bible is true to investigate a story about Jesus' life from the Bible. Assure them you do not intend to pressure them to change their views of the Bible.

2. "Jesus is irrelevant for today." You can respond by accepting their point of view and expressing your perspective such as, "In my studies of the Bible, I've learned much about my everyday relationships from how Jesus related to people in the Bible. Would you want to try looking at one story and see what you think?"

3. "I know nothing about Jesus. I don't want to embarrass myself." Respond by saying, "I'm still learning things myself. Perhaps you would enjoy some passages which illustrate the uniqueness of Jesus? No Bible knowledge is necessary to enjoy discussing one of these studies."

4. "I don't want to be told what to believe. I need to decide for myself." A possible response is, "You are absolutely right—you should decide for yourself. These discussions encourage you to find your own answers and make your own personal decisions."

Adjustments During the Discussion

1. Be mindful of explaining things carefully. The goal is to have them feel "in the know" not "out of it."

2. Ask the Holy Spirit for special help to understand your friend's point of view and questions.

3. Make a greater effort to understand their perspective than to assure they understand yours. This will foster open dialogue and good conversations.

4. Handle the Respond for Life step carefully. Seekers are not familiar with the concept of applying Scripture to our daily lives. They may need just to think about what they have discovered, and this in itself is a marvelous response.

WOMEN OF INFLUENCE:
SERVING MARKETPLACE WOMEN AND CHURCH LEADERS

Women of Influence serves Christian women in the marketplace and church leaders who are ministering to these women through their local church. Today 58 million women are in the marketplace seeking to balance the responsibilities of the office and the home. Christian women desire to balance a third dimension, that of bringing the love of Christ into their work and workplace relationships. By listening to these Christian women, we have discovered that many are eager to find others like themselves who want to live out the gospel in their relationships at work. We have also discovered that those leading ministries to women in their local church are eager to learn how to meet the special needs of marketplace women.

Women of Influence exists to provide resources, personalized ministry consultation, networking opportunities and training to equip church leaders and Christian marketplace women to make a difference for Christ in the mission field of today's marketplace. Meri MacLeod, the series editor for Radical Relationships Bible studies, is associate director of Women of Influence.

WHAT WOMEN OF INFLUENCE OFFERS

- TRAINING SEMINARS addressing a variety of marketplace topics.

- RADICAL RELATIONSHIPS SEMINARS for using these unique Bible studies with a wide variety of people and settings.

- REGIONAL CONFERENCES for spiritual renewal and networking.

- CONSULTATIONS for developing effective ministry strategy.

- "INFLUENCE" NEWSLETTER addressing the special needs of marketplace women and church leaders.

For information on how you or your church can benefit from the training or resources available for the marketplace, contact the Women of Influence at: P.O. Box 6000, Colorado Springs CO 80934. Phone: (719)548-7450. Fax: (719)548-7453. E-mail: mpain@navigato.mhs.compuserve.com

SMALL-GROUP MATERIALS FROM NAVPRESS

BIBLE STUDY SERIES

Design for Discipleship
God in You
God's Design for the Family
Institute of Biblical
  Counseling Series
Learning to Love Series

Lifechange
Love One Another
Radical Relationships
Studies in Christian Living
Thinking Through Discipleship

TOPICAL BIBLE STUDIES

Becoming a Woman of Excellence
Becoming a Woman of Freedom
Becoming a Woman of Purpose
The Blessing Study Guide
Celebrating Life
Homemaking
Intimacy with God
Loving Your Husband

Loving Your Wife
A Mother's Legacy
Praying From God's Heart
Surviving Life in the Fast Lane
To Run and Not Grow Tired
To Walk and Not Grow Weary
What God Does When Men Pray
When the Squeeze Is On

BIBLE STUDIES WITH COMPANION BOOKS

Bold Love
Daughters of Eve
The Discipline of Grace
The Feminine Journey
Inside Out
The Masculine Journey
The Practice of Godliness
The Pursuit of Holiness

Secret Longings of the Heart
Spiritual Disciplines
Tame Your Fears
Transforming Grace
Trusting God
What Makes a Man?
The Wounded Heart
Your Work Matters to God

RESOURCES

Brothers!
How to Build a Small Groups Ministry
How to Lead Small Groups
Jesus Cares for Women
The Navigator Bible Studies
  Handbook

The Small Group Leaders
  Training Course
Topical Memory System
  (KJV/NIV and NASB/NKJV)
Topical Memory System:
  Life Issues

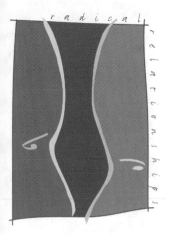

DISCOVER HOW YOU CAN SUCCESSFULLY USE RADICAL RELATIONSHIPS BIBLE STUDIES WITH A WIDE VARIETY OF PEOPLE.

RADICAL RELATIONSHIPS studies are generating new excitement about Bible study. Because they are open-ended, non-threatening, and so easy to use, they appeal to a wide variety of people from many age groups and many walks of life. We'd like to help you get the most out of leading a RADICAL RELATIONSHIPS study by offering you a seminar that is custom-made for your group or church.

Call today to

HERE'S WHAT YOU'LL GET FROM A RADICAL RELATIONSHIPS SEMINAR.

Learn to use RADICAL RELATIONSHIPS studies with:
- college-age to senior adults
- a group of Christians and nonChristians
- neighborhood contacts for church planting
- workplace evangelism or discipleship groups
- church new members classes or home groups
- men's or women's accountability groups

arrange for a

RADICAL RELATIONSHIPS

Find out how you can:
- lead a RADICAL RELATIONSHIPS conversational Bible study without being a Bible teacher
- train others in using RADICAL RELATIONSHIPS Bible studies effectively
- use RADICAL RELATIONSHIPS for evangelism or discipleship
- facilitate discussion and discovery that will keep people coming back for more
- effectively handle difficulties in small-group discussion

seminar tailor-made

THESE SEMINARS ARE CUSTOM-MADE! YOU'LL WORK WITH THE EXPERTS TO SHAPE THE TRAINING THAT FITS THE NEEDS OF YOUR GROUP OR CHURCH.

You decide:
- which training format is best for you (three, four, or six hours)
- which topics you want to address (evangelism, discipleship, training others to use RADICAL RELATIONSHIPS, facilitating effective discussions, a mixture of these topics, or all of them!)
- which audience you want to reach (home groups, church groups, or groups meeting in the marketplace)

to fit your needs!

Call (719) 548-7450.